The Complete Book
Of Beer Drinking Games

(and other really important stuff)

"You can only drink 30 or 40 glasses of beer a day, no matter how rich you are."

Col. Adolphus Busch

THE COMPLETE BOOK OF *BEER*
DRINKING GAMES

(and other really important stuff)

Andy Griscom, Ben Rand, and Scott Johnston

Mustang Publishing
New Haven

Cover design by Deborah Daley
Interior design by Rollin Riggs

Library of Congress Cataloging in Publication Data:
Griscom, Andy, 1960-
  The complete book of beer drinking games, and other really important stuff.

  1. Drinking games—United States. 2. Beer. 3. United States—Social conditions—1980-   —Anecdotes, facetiae, satire, etc. 4. College students—United States—Anecdotes, facetiae, satire, etc. I. Rand, Ben, 1960-   . II. Johnston, Scott, 1960-
III. Title.
GV1202.D74G75 1983   793.2   84-2024
ISBN 0-914457-01-2 (pbk.)

10 9

PICTURE CREDITS: pg. 14, Wide World; pg. 15, UPI; pg. 26, UPI; pgs. 41 and 42, David Ottenstein; pg. 62, courtesy Earthwatch; pg. 84, courtesy Heineken Breweries; pg. 98, Wide World; pg. 116, courtesy Universal Studios; pg. 126, Rollin Riggs.

Drawings on pages 25, 31, 34, 35, 54, 59, 60, 68, 97, 101, 113, 115, 124 by SEAN KELLY.

All other art from *The Dover Book of Food and Drink*.

Dedicated to our parents, for funding
four years of research

Acknowledgements

We have had a great deal of help putting this book together. In particular, we would like to thank Harold and Lucille Morowitz for all their help and advice. Special thanks also to Eric Mogilnicki and George Shepherd for their excellent contributions.

We would also like to thank the following: Jake Jacobsen, Chris Jorden, Chris Cummings, Drew Lieberman, Pat Conran, John Garber, Charlie Clarke, Michael Clark, Andy Waugh, Mike Aubrey, Ray Small, Scott Gelband, Sarah, Jim, Fred, and Chuck Buffum, Bill Glynn, Sim Johnston, Dorothy Shaw, Ben Davol, Lawrence Callahan, Leo and Brian, Bart Enders, Joe Romano, Caitlin Doyle, Bruce Jacobsen, Rollin Riggs, Michel le Ventripotent, Mike Natan, Jake Smith, Malcolm MacLear, Loryn and Kim, Rich Smith, Ted Berenblum, Whitney Sander, Doc-oh! Burke, Bob Hallifax, Fred Loney, Dave Winans, Andy Kaplan, Dave Tohir, Todd Wadd, Gretchen Knapp, Steve Zuckerman, Mike Balay, George Johnston, Tom Hawkins, Mark Bolender, Telly Jorden, Alexa, Lizey, and El, Delta Kappa Epsilon, U. of Michigan School of Music, the Mesopotamians for inventing beer, Henry Ford for inventing the car, and Smith College for giving us an excuse to road trip.

DON'T DRIVE DRUNK

Do we really need to tell you not to drink and drive?

Damn right we do! The National Transportation Safety Board estimates that almost **half of all fatal traffic accidents involve drunk drivers**. That means that these cretins caused about 22,000 deaths in 1982 alone. It is even worse in the 16-24 age group, where alcohol related crashes are the **leading cause of death**.

It takes very little alcohol to affect your driving. A mere four drinks can seriously impair the reflexes of a 220-pound football player. So imagine what a few drinks could do to a 140-pound lightweight like yourself.

Now, we realize that you are not stupid (after all, you popped five bucks for this book), but do not think for a second that this book encourages you to play beer games and then drive. If you do, you are a total loser and you should be in jail. When we road trip, for example, the driver is forbidden to drink. After all, the object of road-tripping is to get there in one piece.

If you want to kill yourself, do everyone a favor and play with a toaster in the bathtub. Just don't drink and drive.

Table of Contents

Introduction 11
A Few Words About Life, Love, and Beer 13
Gaming Etiquette 17
The Mung Rag 19
Our Favorite Swill Beers 21
Snarfing, Booting, and Reverse Drinking 22
The Boot Factor 24

Boot Factor One 25
General Hover • Indian Sweat • Beer 99 •
The Muffin Man • Killer • Burn-Out • Stack-a-Brew

Boot Factor Two 35
Chug Boat/Hi Bob • Famous Names • Thumper •
Tang • Boat Racing • Beer Shooting
• Fuzzy Duck • Beer Softball • Categories •
Beergammon • Beer Checkers • Pookie

Beer Finishing School 52
The Beer Years 55
The Road Trip 56

Boot Factor Three 59
Beer Golf • Whales Tails • Bullshit • Frisbeer
• Dunk the Duchess • Swim Relays • Mexican •
Quarters • Cups • I Never • Zoom, Schwartz,
Perfigliano • Fizz Buzz • Cardinal Puff

The Beer Curriculum

History 124 83
Biology 450 86
Biology Lab 101 88
Music 420 90
Sociology 125 93
English 202 95

Boot Factor Four 97
*Beer-an-Inning • Shot-a-Minute • Yards • Caps
• Acey-Deucey • Hi-Lo • Red-Black • Dimes •
Beer Pong • Volley Pong • Blow Pong • Bladder Bust*

Boot Factor Five 115
*Beer Hunter • Slush Fund • Kill the Keg •
Tending the Teat • The 100 Beer Club • Boot-a-Bout*

You Can Help 127

Introduction

Hi there! Welcome to an enthusiastic and somewhat irreverent look at college, America, parties, and mostly, beer. We call this book irreverent because it is. We are direct and simple in our writing, and we pull no punches. We do not let our descriptions of beer-gaming get mired in a bog of euphemistic rhetoric. If we wrote in more conventional — some would say less offensive — language, the very spirit which we seek to capture would be lost. After all, when you're drinking with some buddies at a bar and one of them is about to lose it, do you say, "Caution, friends, Joe is preparing to regurgitate!" Of course not. You'd say, "Heads up! Joe's gonna blow chow!" So that's what we'll say in the book, too.

This is not to imply that America's youth are a besotted mass of ill-mannered trouble-makers. To the contrary, today's beer drinker is outgoing, spirited, and patriotic. In short, a real swell person. Despite occasional animalistic behavior, the beer drinker today has only the best of intentions.

Now, about beer games. Most of you have played them and enjoyed yourself quite a bit. But during our three years of research, we discovered that even the most hard-core partiers didn't know more than a handful of games. So in the interest of Science and in the hopes of creating more fun for the world, we have catalogued over 50 beer games, which we present, with complete rules and descriptions, herein.

Although our efforts were thorough, we are sure that there are more games out there, and if we can come up with 50 more, we'll probably get around to writing a sequel — *Beneath the Planet of the Beer Games*, or something. We'd greatly appreciate your help in this vital project, so if you know of more great drinking games, please drop us a line in care of the publisher, and we'll send you an autographed barf bag, or something really nice like that. (And, of course, we'll put your name in the next book.) In fact, we consider it our patriotic duty to continue to catalog drinking games. After all, do the Soviets have a book like this? No way, chief. This is a tough job, but hey, somebody's got to do it.

In addition to all the beer games, you'll find many essays, observations, cartoons, and other stuff that some ignorant people might call "filler." Those people would be sadly mistaken, though, for the true beer gamesman knows that drinkers do not live on games alone. The passion for beer drinking touches all facets of life. Some of the chapters, like "The Road Trip," are related to beer drinking mostly in a spiritual way. Other subjects, such as fern bars, don't really have much to do with beer at all, except that we happen to like beer and dislike fern bars for much the same reasons. And, besides, we just felt like writing about them.

We think the book is really pretty funny. It gets us psyched, and we hope it gets you psyched, too. If you like it, you'll have some good laughs, learn some new games, and have more fun at the next party you go to. If you don't like it, you'll probably get pretty upset. But that's okay, too, because then maybe you'll sue us, and we'll get lots of free publicity. In any case, let's get on with the fun.

Andy Griscom
Ben Rand
Scott Johnston

October, 1983

A Few Words About Life, Love and Beer

Time was, drinking beer was "uncool," or worse, "square." Smoking pot was "in" on college campuses in the 60's and early 70's, along with Army fatigues, long hair, and minimal hygiene. The surge in the popularity of marijuana was really a matter of convenience for yesterday's youth: you could get high and make a political statement at the same time. Like Woodstock and rock music, smoking pot was part celebration and part protest.

But that's all passed. Our generation was oblivious to the problems of those years, being preoccupied with Little League and long division. Now, Vietnam is history, and the flower child generation has grown up to become stockbrokers and advertising executives.

And, praise be, beer is back.

The turning point was the presidency of Gerald R. Ford. Unlike his predecessors, President Ford was a man you could imagine sharing a six-pack with. Lyndon Johnson invited defiance, from the burning of draft cards to the burning of joints. (Besides, he drank Fresca.) And Richard Nixon incited paranoia — it took a strong belt of hard liquor to get him off your mind.

*Billy Carter: the only brother
of a President to have a beer named for him*

But Jerry, he was like a favorite uncle — perhaps not so bright, but a certifiably good guy, and you just knew he could drink a beer. America's basic values, questioned by events here and half a world away, were beginning to reassert themselves. We could be glad to be Americans again, and happy to hoist a beer to Our Pal the President.

The true watershed, however, was the Carter Administration. Although Jimmy reminded one of Milk of Magnesia, what world leader has ever had a beer named after his brother? When Billy Carter joined the pantheon of all-time swillers, beer had re-entered the American mainstream. And today, President Reagan, though a bit too old to get psyched for a good round of Slush Fund, continues to show that beer is integral to the American Way of Life. After a hard day battling Tip O'Neill and riding horses, what else *could* he drink but a cold brewski?

Beer hasn't changed; we have. Being "square" or "establishment" doesn't seem so bad anymore, and America realizes that it's okay to appreciate your parents, your country, and the golden nectar of America's heartland, beer.

President Reagan hoists a cold one in a Boston bar.

No regrets here: the resurgence of beer is a happy sign. Beer binds parent to child, worker to worker, and student to student. Beer is American, not imported, like drugs. Beer is the drink America comes home to, the drink of hometowns, backyard barbecues, and a night out with the gang. Beer is for before, during, and after the game, any game. Beer takes the agony from defeat and adds the thrill to victory.

There's another great thing about beer — bars. In almost every town from Wabash to Walla Walla, places exist for only one reason: to create a pleasant environment for socking down a couple of frosties. Other things, like peanuts, Monday Night Football, and jukeboxes, just seem to contribute to the taste of that cold one in your hand.

But the best thing about beer, as we will go to great lengths to show, is that it can be used to play drinking games. These games have become the rage of collegiate America, practically wiping out the existence of 8 a.m. classes. In fact, it was our hope that this book might be distributed at orientation to all college students with other essentials such as course listings, school regulations, and meal contracts. Much to our surprise, every registrar we contacted flatly refused. (Some, however, did express interest in adding it to their own personal libraries.)

Of course, we do not advocate beer drinking as a solution to problems or an escape from life. We argue only that beer drinking can be fun and is, well, American. After all, even George Washington spent his spare time at Mount Vernon brewing his own brand of ale.

In short, when America feels good about itself, it drinks beer, and drinking beer helps America feel good about itself. Enjoying the golden brew is our generation's way of following that great American tradition of exuberance. It is our hope that we have captured this spirit in the pages that follow.

Cheers!

Gaming Etiquette

To tell you the truth, beer etiquette is a contradiction in terms. Beer games are often rude, and players even ruder. In an attempt to curb such incivility, an altogether arbitrary set of rules has evolved among veteran beer gamers. Well, actually, the real point is that the more rules players have to obey, the more infractions they make, and the more beer they drink. And this, after all, is the whole idea in the first place.

Beer-gaming etiquette varies from one geo-political area to another, indeed from one game to another. There are, however, as many as ten rules players can choose to play by.

Rule #1: No Pointing. Since pointing is one of the most common things to do, especially when identifying players who blunder, there naturally must be a rule against it. Anyone who points with his finger must take a swig from his beer. The only acceptable way to point is with a bent elbow.*

Rule #2: No "Drink"-ing. Whenever a player uses the word "drink" in any form (e.g., drinking, drunk, drank, drinked, drinkly, etc.) he must drink — er, imbibe.

Rule #3: Wrong Hands. Right-handed players are forbidden to drink with their right hands, and left-handed players with their left. For the hard-core, there is no drinking with either hand. Any time a player is caught infringing, he must drink again. Incidentally, it is considered poor sportsmanship to sit on your drinking hand or tape it to your leg.

Rule #4: No Swearing. This needs no explanation, but it's a real killer.

Rule #5: The Ten Minute Warning. In addition to the "no pointing" rule, this is considered a standard regulation.

---

*This practice originated with the game Whales Tails. The idea is that whales don't have fingers, so they would have to point with a flipper. When a human points with his elbow, it resembles a whale pointing with his flipper. Sort of.

Players must give a ten minute warning before quitting a beer game. This prevents a player who just lost big from welching on his debts by claiming he hears his mother calling and dashing off, leaving the five beers he was supposed to chug.

Rule #6: No Pronouns. This is one of the most difficult rules. By excluding pronouns from a game, players will get confused when they try to identify each other. This leads them to point, and so they violate Rule #1, and so they drink.

Rule #7: First Infraction. If a player makes a mistake and the game continues for a while before players realize the infraction, any blunders subsequent to the original are forgiven.

Rule #8: Discrete Digit. During the course of a game, a player can discretely hang his forefinger off the edge of the table. Players who see this quietly do the same as they continue to play the game. The last player to hang his digit drinks.

Rule #9: Golden Chair. Before a player leaves the game to go to the bathroom for a visit with Captain Leaky or for a casual reverse drink, he must say "golden chair" to gain immunity from being called while absent. This rule is a must in verbal tag games in which players "away on business" often get called mistakenly.

Rule #10: Point of Order. Unless you are still in the 8th Grade, you will rarely have parents around to supervise your beer games and make impartial rulings. So, the Point of Order establishes an "in-house" Tribunal to settle arguments, clarify rules, and make additions to a game. When a problem arises, a player simply yells, "Point of Order!" All players point their elbows into the air and yell in response, "Point of Order!" They then put their fists in the middle of the table with their thumbs sticking out sideways. The player who initiated the Point of Order states what the players are voting on — say, to introduce a new rule, decide on an old one, or determine whether a player should be allowed to go to the bathroom. He then yells "Vote!" and the players either point their thumbs up for approval or down for denial. A denied motion is accompanied by a loud buzzing sound by the whole Tribunal (just like when the fat lady loses on *The Price Is Right*).

The Mung Rag

The Mung Rag is a beer-gaming essential. It is no more than an old towel, bathrobe, or pair of boxer shorts, used to wipe up the spills and whatever that inevitably occur in the course of an evening of beer-gaming. Hence, the Mung Rag's other name, the "Table Zamboni." (A Zamboni, for those of you who grew up in the Third World or Texas and haven't watched a whole lot of hockey, is the machine which glides over the ice in a hockey rink between periods, smoothing and re-surfacing the ice.)

To us, however, the Mung Rag is much more: it is a friend and a trusted companion. One Mung Rag should last up to a full year. It should never be thrown away after a party. Rather, let your Mung Rag bide its time between beery evenings under your couch or bed, or in a corner of the bathroom, preferably near a collection of dust balls. Try to develop a strong relationship with your Mung Rag, and let its gentle aroma serve as a reminder of the great parties past.

If your Mung Rag should ever need washing — like when it attracts the attention of local health officials — place it, by itself, in an industrial-size washer with bleach, detergent, and plenty of antibiotics. Good luck.

Thirty Synonyms For "Beer"

1. brew
2. brewski
3. brewage
4. brew dogger
5. milk
6. golden nectar
7. nectar of the gods
8. juice
9. sauce
10. goon
11. beevo
12. brew-hah
13. suds
14. 12-ounce weight
15. grog
16. swill
17. pop
18. roadies
19. chilly
20. stew
21. frosty
22. shooter
23. toby
24. caker
25. liquid courage
26. pounder
27. tweeners
28. pony (8 ounces)
29. screaming green meanies
30. green dragon

Our Favorite Swill Beers

Since beer games obviously involve substantial amounts of beer, the frequent gamester will find it desirable to use economical brands. After all, you just don't chug Heineken. It's also a good idea to use beers that are at least remotely palatable. Enthusiasm for a good round of Thumper wanes quickly if the only brew anyone can find is an old case cf "Wild Mustang."

The following is a list of brands that we believe best combine economy and taste for gaming purposes: Narragansett, Old Milwaukee, Piels Real Draft, Blatz, Schaefer, Ortlieb's (Joe's Beer), Rolling Rock, Rainier, Utica Club, Pearl, Black Label, Dixie.

Black Label, six-packs of which are known to veteran gamesters as "Black Labs," is our favorite. It can often be found (warm) for $5.00 a case. Calling cases of Black Label "kennels" is key.

One last word about swill beers: sometimes you will want to play with a beer that doesn't even make the first gesture toward good taste. You see, a beer that tastes really foul can make your games much more manly, because everyone gets to prove to each other how much punishment he can take. We have found Wiedeman's and Genesee Cream Ale particularly well-suited for this purpose. Imagine losing a long round of Beer Hunter with Genesee. Now that's *tough*. Other possibilities include Olde English "800," Colt 45, and Iron City.

"There is no bad beer:
some kinds are better than others."
— German Proverb

Snarfing, Booting, and Reverse Drinking

Defining the Terms

Let's face it, regurgitation is a delicate subject. No doubt there are those who prefer that we didn't discuss it. However, we feel that if Cathy Rigby can talk about feminine hygiene on television, we can discuss booting.

Despite many subtle distinctions and nuances, there are really only three types of regurgitation: snarfing, booting, and reverse drinking. Each may be encountered from time to time by the serious beer-gamesman, so some clarification is in order.

Snarfing: A snarf is definitely undesirable. It represents failure. Snarfing occurs when someone attempts, unsuccessfully, to chug a beer. Usually, the unfortunate drinker pours beer into his mouth faster than it can be swallowed. As a result, the beer must seek an alternate exit, and much of it will find its way into the olfactory passages and out the nose. While spectators may find this amusing, it is, on the whole, an unpleasant experience.

Booting: Booting is something we are all familiar with. Euphemistically known as "throwing-up," booting even happens to non-gamesters when they get sick. Since it involves liquids and solids that have begun the grand tour of the digestive tract, booting is by far the most wrenching form of regurgitation. Visual reminders of recent meals one did not care to see again are often included.

Reverse Drinking: Also known as "blowing foam," reverse drinking is the least unpleasant type of regurgitation. Actually, it is a drinking tactic more than a drinking mishap. It enables one to continue beer-gaming long after the stomach says "No."

Simply put, reverse drinking is ejecting that which you have only just begun to consume. Ideally, the time between consumption and ejection (known as the "lag time") is the time it takes to reach the bathroom. Unfortunately, the lag time is often too short for a player to run downstairs and find an empty stall. The process is painless and allows at least one more round of Boot-a-Bout or Blow Pong. Those with a scientific bent are fascinated to find that their recently discarded beer is still foamy, while dieters appreciate all those foregone calories.

There really is something about drinking games that brings out the best in a person — literally. Puking is a classic victim of bad press. Constant negative publicity about blowing chow has created a vicious circle: people don't look forward to upchucking, so they don't enjoy it when they do. So, let's look at some of the advantages:

The best thing about woofing is that it makes room for more beer. The advantages of this are self-evident.

Another positive aspect is a little less obvious. Did you know that stomach muscles never get tighter than when you're booting? That's right, booting is great exercise! (Look for our work-out book soon.)

A final attribute of booting is that it makes for great stories. This makes you a popular-kind-of-person at parties. What member of the opposite sex doesn't love a rousing tale about blowing doughnuts?

By now, you should be convinced that booting can be a positive experience. If not, there are additional physical, spiritual, and philosophical reasons for not minding an occasional heave. First, the act is, by definition, physically beneficial; your body responsibly decides against keeping that last beer. Secondly, if you can free your mind of societal indoctrination, losing your lunch can be a moving, spiritual experience. All at once, your body is poised in a moment of great catharsis. There is a sudden sense of complete abandon to a force greater than yourself, and then a profound quiet. Finally, throwing up recalls basic philosophical questions. After a chunder, is your stomach half full or half empty?

The Boot Factor

(a.k.a. Earl Indicator, Ralph Rating, Vomit Vector)

The Boot Factor, based on a scale from one to five, indicates the level of havoc a beer game will wreak upon your system. The Boot Factor rates a beer game's inherent capacity to stimulate a little-known area in the brain, the *regurgitus violentus locii*. Simply put, a Boot Factor of 1 describes the lowest potential for tossing cookies, while a Boot Factor of 5 warns of an almost assured heave.*

However, the Boot Factor should be considered as more than just a guidline. Used wisely, it can provide essential pre-game information which you should use to plot strategy. For example, in a game with a low Boot Factor, concentrate on ways to defeat fellow players by using your intellect, such as it may be. But after a few rounds of a high-factor game, very little intellect remains, so players must focus on immediate physical concerns ("How big is my stomach?") and reserve thoughts on strategy for less cerebral matters ("Where is the closest toilet?").

For over-achievers, the Boot Factor provides a numerical incentive for consuming massive quantities of brew. Tell your bookworm friend that the Boot Factor can be compared to his G.P.A., with five being the equivalent of the *summa cum laude* of beer-gaming. The knowledge that one is a regular upper-level competitor can do wonders for the ego, not to mention attract countless fawning members of the opposite sex.

Use the Boot Factor strictly for comparison. Volume and frequency of gastro-intestinal evacuations may vary with length of game and size of penalty. Your actual game mileage may be less.

Boot Factor One

Games rated Boot Factor One consist of a varied selection for the beginner who yearns for the excitement and camaraderie of beer-gaming, without the forced consumption of entire pitchers at a time. B.F. 1 games serve as an introduction to the world of hard-core gamesters, a preliminary step for the neophyte in quest of the upper echelons of beer-gaming. For experienced players, the Boot Factor One games serve as limbering exercises for the more demanding games to follow.

General Hover
Indian Sweat
Beer 99
The Muffin Man
Killer
Burn-Out
Stack-a-Brew

Even President Reagan
enjoys a good round of General Hover

1.

General Hover

Boot Factor: 1

Also known as "Hovering Bunnies," **General Hover** is so cute that even Mr. Rogers enjoys a round now and then.

The game begins with a "general hover" — everyone holds out his hands palms down, and shakes them. One player initiates the action by clasping his hands together and pointing at another player. The second player must then make Mickey Mouse ears. The player on "Mickey's" right makes a right-handed Mickey, and the player on the left makes a left-handed Mickey.

All three "Mickeys" must be made nearly simultaneously. Any delay causes the delaying player to drink.

After holding these positions for a second or two, the player making the "full Mickey" says, "General hover," and everyone begins hovering again. After an indeterminate period, the Mickey clasps and points to another player, who then becomes the new Mickey. This continues until someone messes up.

There is also a maneuver called the "jockey." Anyone may call a "jockey" at any time during the game, except when players are Mickeying. When a jockey is called, everyone jumps up and slaps his hands on his thighs, making a sound like a galloping horse. The person who initiated the jockey ends it simply by sitting down and announcing a return to "general hover." There is little purpose to a jockey except to make any women playing jump up and down.

Because **General Hover** is so cute, it is more often enjoyed by women than men. Most men wouldn't be caught dead making Mickey Mouse ears, unless of course they are trying to make "Mickey" with one of the Minnie Mice.

2.

Indian Sweat

Boot Factor: 1

Indian Sweat is a gambling game, not unlike poker. However, in **Indian Sweat**, the stakes are much loftier, since players bet beer, not money.

Each player is dealt one card, face down. Players are not allowed to look at their cards. Instead, they must bring the card to their foreheads without looking at the card's face. Thus, a player can see everyone's card but his own.

Bidding commences. The dealer begins, and the rest of the players take turns betting any number of shots of beer that the card on their own foreheads is the highest in the group.

As the "pot" increases, the players who feel their cards might be losers drop out. They must then drink the amount of beer in the "pot." At the end of the betting, the player with the lowest card must drink the final amount bid.

"Now for drinks, now for some dancing with a good beat."

— Horace (65-8 B.C.), xxxvii

3.
Beer 99

Boot Factor: 1

Earlier, we implied that beer-drinking builds character. Well, not **Beer 99**. The object of the game is not to drink, but to cheat.

Beer 99 is a card game in which deception and sleazy tactics succeed, and honesty often fails. Each player is dealt four cards. The value of a card is the same as in blackjack: aces are one or eleven, face cards are ten, and all others are the value shown. The first player throws one card face up on the discard pile and announces the value of his card. The next player then plays a card and announces the sum of his card plus the first.

The game continues in this fashion, with each player adding his card's value to the total. The object is to build the pile until it totals 99. When this happens, the person next in rotation must drink. If a player discards and sends the pile value over 99, then he must drink.

Fortunately, there are several ways to avoid topping 99. By the rules, kings, tens, and fours all have special properties. A king can give the total of 99 to anyone the player choses. A ten lowers or raises the count by ten, so someone who gets 99 can play a ten and announce 89 to avoid drinking. A four allows you to skip a turn: if a player receives 99 he can play a four and pass the 99 to the next player. When 99 is reached, the cards are reshuffled if necessary, and the pile value starts over at zero.

A player must drink if it comes his turn to discard and he has no cards left. So, to keep a full hand, a player should always draw after playing a card. The only time you're permitted to draw is immediately after your discard, so stay alert.

Now, about cheating. This is where most of the fun and skill come into **Beer 99**. A good cheater will always have a large supply of cards in hand, shoe, sleeve, sock, etc. He can get them from anywhere. The easiest place is from the draw pile. Deft players will also pilfer two or three cards from the discard pile or from fellow players. Players may also miscalculate the pile total as they discard.

If a player is accused of cheating, the others vote on his guilt or innocence. If more than half the players register "thumbs down," the accused must drink. Otherwise, all those showing thumbs up drink for their false accusation. Cheating infractions tend to increase as a game continues into the night and alcohol obliterates any sense of integrity.

"They drink with impunity, or anybody who invites them."

— Artemus Ward

4.
Muffin Man

Boot Factor: 1

Mother Goose will be turning over in her grave when she hears about this one. But she won't be the only one who's spinning.

In **Muffin Man**, two players each balance a full cup of beer on their heads. They then begin to recite in unison a nursery rhyme in loud, obnoxious voices. The first blockhead whose beer falls off his head not only gets wet but also must chug the victor's beer.

5.
Killer

Boot Factor: 1

In no way related to Kill the Keg, a Boot Factor 5 game, **Killer** is a card game with drinking applications.

All players are dealt one card face down. One of these cards must be an ace, and the player who receives the ace is the "killer." His mission is to assassinate the other players one at a time by winking discretely at each of them. He must not let anyone but his victim see the wink. Once a player has been "killed" by the wink, he declares himself dead and, to insure that he will rest in peace, he must chug his beer. Dying is always a dramatic event and involves moaning, clutching at the throat, and generally hamming it up.

If another player sees the assassin winking at someone else, he may accuse the "killer." If the accusation is correct, the "killer" must chug a beer for each player left alive. The cards are then collected, and another round begins. If the accusation is false, the accusing player downs a penalty drink and promptly dies. Before giving up the ghost, he must also take his R.I.P. chug.

6.
Burn-Out

Boot Factor: 1

Burn-Out involves the use of a lit cigarette. This is not to say that the game is only played by smokers. In fact, many times we abstainers have bummed a cigarette from some incredulous bar patron so we could get in a couple of rounds of **Burn-Out**. Smokers can't believe we use their precious butts in this way. Tough.

The other equipment necessary to play **Burn-Out** is a glass (preferably short with a wide mouth) and a napkin. Put a single layer of the napkin over the glass and pull it down around the sides. Next, wet the napkin around the rim of the glass and tear off the excess, so the napkin covers only the mouth of the glass. The final set-up will look like a miniature bongo drum. Then take a dime and gently lay it in the center of the napkin. Now you're ready to begin.

To play, participants take turns burning holes in the napkin around the dime with the cigarette. Whoever burns the hole that causes the dime to fall must drink (from another glass, of course — we discovered that drinking ashes really blows.)

Burn-Out has such a low Boot Factor because it can take an amazingly long time for the dime to fall. This, however, is why the game is fun. The dime often becomes suspended on the tiniest strip of paper, and deciding where to burn the next hole can be a real challenge.

We highly recommend **Burn-Out** for the bar scene. You always make lots of new friends because everyone wonders what the hell you're doing and comes over to ask. **Burn-Out** is also the perfect game to play when you're warming down after a night of intense beer-gaming.

7.
Stack-a-Brew

Boot Factor: 1

Stack-a-Brew is the game to play on Saturday night with Friday night's empties. As you may have guessed, the idea is to take turns stacking cans end on end until they topple. It's really more fun than an Erector Set, or even Mr. Potato Head. The uncoordinated sap who is responsible for the crash, drinks.

The beauty of this game is that the more you play, the more cans you have to play with.

Boot Factor Two

The Boot Factor Two games teach fundamental principles of beer-gaming while still boasting a low boot potential. The gamester can acquire and polish the skills that form the basis of survival in most upper-level games: mastering the unique verbal and non-verbal language associated with beer-gaming; knowing whom *not* to sit next to (lightweights are always the first to lose it); and training the bladder to retain many more ounces of beer than it was ever meant to hold.

Chug Boat/Hi Bob
Famous Names
Thumper
Tang
Boat Racing
Beer Shooting
Fuzzy Duck
Beer Softball
Categories
Beergammon
Beer Checkers
Pookie

Eighteen Things To Look For In a Truly Classic Bar

1. Juke box (rock, Motown, Sinatra, no disco)
2. Cheap pitchers
3. Walls cluttered with collegiate memorabilia
4. Bathroom has no locks, no toilet paper, and no running water
5. No waitresses or service of any kind
6. Munchies available (especially hard-boiled eggs, beer nuts, and pretzels)
7. Tables made of carvable wood with lots of initials carved in
8. Real, old-fashioned pinball machines
9. No hanging plants
10. Bushes outside for late-night watering
11. Pizza available nearby
12. Six-foot TV screen (optional)
13. Greasy fries and burgers served all night
14. Equally greasy bartenders
15. Pay telephone available to wake-up wimp roommates
16. Lots of happy hours and beer specials
17. Broken neon sign
18. Menthol odor from sanitary pucks (a.k.a. urinal candy) noticeable throughout establishment

8.
Chug Boat

Boot Factor: 2

Now, we know that no one really plans to watch *Love Boat*, right? But just in case you turn it on by accident and start getting confused by the plot, at least you can do the sensible thing and crack open a couple of sixes.

Playing **Chug Boat** is as easy as some of the guest stars on the show. Each player chooses a "regular" (the Captain, Doc, Gofer, Julie, Vicki, or Isaac), and the player drinks whenever his character appears on the screen. The boat itself is also considered a viable character. Players choosing the *Pacific Princess* must drink each time there is a full-length shot of the boat. If one of the story lines revolves around your character, you'll begin to think you really are on some kind of cruise.

There's only one more rule: whenever there's a gratuitous shot of a well-endowed female sauntering across the deck, everyone must yell "Balloon smugglers!" and drink.

If **Chug Boat** is played during a two-hour special, it is more appropriately called "Love Boot."

Hi Bob

For videophiles who are not satisfied with just Chug Boat, there is **Hi Bob**.

Hi Bob is played while watching *The Bob Newhart Show*. The only rules are that everyone must drink half a glass of beer whenever a character says "Bob," and chug a full glass when a character says "Hi, Bob."

Sound easy? Guess again. It's just amazing how television screenwriters create scripts with drinking games in mind.

9.
Famous Names

Boot Factor: 2

The next time someone accuses you, a dedicated beer gamester, of being ignorant about current events, grab your drinking buddies, tap a keg, and ask this bonehead to play **Famous Names**. He will soon realize he was wrong: beer drinkers can be really well-informed people.

One player starts by saying the first and last name of a "famous" person — that is, a well-known living, dead, or fictitious character. The next player must name a famous person whose first name begins with the first letter of the previous famous person's last name. Got it? The game continues around the circle in this way, and the doofus who cannot come up with a new name in a few seconds must drink and start the new round.

For example, a fairly impressive round might go like this: Thurston Howell, Herman Munster, Marcia Brady, Beaver Cleaver, Charles Bronson, Barney Rubble, Rosie Grier, George Jetson, John Kennedy, Kyle Rote, Jr., Richard Nixon, Norman Mailer, and so on.

Hook the beer-gaming skeptic on **Famous Names**, and it should be no problem to lure him into Quarters, Boot-a-Bout, and other *really* meaningful pursuits. And any parent, employer, or academician will certainly be impressed by the demonstration of your knowledge of the world around you in this game. At the very least, it proves that you read *People* magazine the last time you were at the dentist.

(Hint: the names "Johnny Quest" and "Efram Zimbalist, Jr." are almost sure winners.)

10.
Thumper

Boot Factor: 2

Thumper is essentially a tag game with sign language. Each player chooses a simple sign which can be made with one or two hands: tugging the ear, thumbs up, the "O.K." sign, etc.

To begin, players sit in a circle and begin "thumping" in a rhythmic fashion. Players slap both hands twice against their thighs or the table, then clap their hands twice, and repeat. The player starting the round makes his sign during the two slapping beats and then the sign of another player on the clapping beats. Whoever's sign was just introduced must make his sign during the next slapping beats, and then the sign of yet another player on the claps.

The difficulty lies in tying this together: recognizing your sign, remembering the sign of another player, while maintaining the beat. At all times, anyone not signing must be thumping. Players drink when they are incapable of signing to the beat or when they make the sign of the player who has just made their sign. A fast beat can make **Thumper** a particularly devastating game.

Thumper is well-suited for boy-girl or fraternity-sorority contests, especially when obscene signs are used. If the right signals are sent, who knows? A little one-on-one **Thumper** may follow the game.

11.
Tang

Boot Factor: 2

Invented by Yale students in the 1940's, **Tang** is a venerable team drinking sport, and it has nothing to do with the space-age orange juice of the same name. To spectators, the game looks like just another chugging match, but its many technical and strategic nuances make it something much more. At Yale, teams practice for the entire school year before they go head-to-head in a wet, beer-inhaling showdown.

Two teams of ten must line up on opposite sides of a long table. In front of each player rest two eight-ounce glasses of beer filled to the brim. Each player assumes the Tanging position beneath the table. A referee dips his thumb up to the first knuckle into each glass to assure that all are equally full. (As the referee submerges his thumb, beer should flow freely over the rim of the glass. If not, he adds more beer and re-tests the glass.)

After checking all the glasses and asking the players if they are ready, the referee announces "practice taps" and raps an empty bottle on the table three times slowly and rhythmically. He then says "real thing" and taps three times again at the same pace.

On the third tap, two time-keepers start their stopwatches, and the first drinker on each team chugs his first glass of beer. When the glass is empty, the player must slam it down on the table, thus signaling to the next team member to chug his first glass. When the second player slams his glass, the third chugs, and so on down the line.

As the glasses pound down along the table, the race will approach the tenth player, who is known as the "corner man." This player should be the swiftest drinker on the team, because he must down *both* his beers, one after the other. After the corner man finishes his second beer, the race reverses direction and goes back up the line — player #9 must

A Tang match at Yale

drink his second beer, then #8, and so on.

When the first players from each team — the guys who started it all in the first place — slam down their glasses, the time-keepers stop their watches and note the elapsed time. The first team to finish is unofficially declared the winner.

However, before he can announce the true victor, the referee must check each drinker for infractions and assess any penalties, and this is where the *quality* of the chug becomes a factor. If the drinker has spilled, snarfed, or left in his glass more than a tablespoonful of beer, he is declared a "gross wet,"and the referee adds three penalty seconds onto his team's time. If the drinker has left or spilled less than a tablespoonful, he is declared a "wet," and the referee penalizes his team one-and-a-half seconds. But if the player drank everything and spilled nothing, the referee calls "clean drink" and assesses no penalty.

Hence, a speedy chugger averaging one second per beer can ruin his once superb time with two gross wets, and thus sink his team. A moderately paced, clean drinking team will almost always beat a fast, wet one.

Though veteran Tangers appear nonchalant as they swallow an eight-ounce brew in under a second, these quaffers have perfected their art through hard practice and a knowledgeable use of the tricks of the trade. Careful study of these athletes can only help the beginning Tanger. Here are some specific suggestions:

Before the race, the beer must be warmed to room temperature and de-carbonated by shaking or stirring (those chilly little bubbles cause many an unnecessary snarf). Wet the front of your shirt so that any spillage won't be so noticeable to the referee. Position your body under the table and your chin right on the edge so you can really throw your head all the way back. Keeping low gives the glass less distance to travel, and saves crucial milliseconds. It's also important to exhale immediately before your chug, thus preventing your esophagus from being constricted by your air-filled lungs.

Above all, relax. Nervousness tightens the throat and makes for an unsteady hand, the downfall of many a would-be Tanger. You must establish an intimate relationship with your beer. Let yourself become one with the liquid before you, so that Tanging becomes a swift, natural act. Watching *Kung Fu* before your match also helps.

The "corner man"
must tang his two beers consecutively.

12.
Boat Racing

Boot Factor: 2

In essence, **Boat Racing** is the British version of Tang. Since it requires only players and beer — the lowest common denominator of beer gaming — it is a perfect drinking game for a bar. **Boat Racing** is especially suited for the crew jocks in the crowd.

Each team of nine people lines up in the fashion of a crew in its shell. That is, eight players stand in a single file line, and the smallest (or lightest) member of the team — known as the "coxswain" — stands at the front of the line, facing the others.

Each member of the "boat" has a full mug of brew, and the race begins with the coxswain, who chugs his beer as fast as he can. When he is finished, he places his glass upside-down on his head, thus signaling the next man in line (the first person facing the cox) to chug. When this man is finished, he too inverts his glass on his head, and the man behind him starts to chug, and so on down the line. The team which gets to the end of its "boat" first is the winner. (Remember that it is the duty of the cox to pace his team by shouting "Stroke! Stroke!" and to encourage them by yelling "Power chug!" at crucial moments.)

Inverting your cup on your head assures everyone that you have indeed finished your beer. For us Americans, a few ounces of brew on the scalp hardly seems a severe penalty. But remember, this is a British game, and the Limeys are a tad on the daintier side.

Those who are especially outrageous will realize that it is quite legal if each team member simply pours his beer on his head without bothering to drink any of it. Though we consider this waste sinful, you can beat the other "boats" by lengths with this method. This trick works well once, maybe twice, a night.

After real crew races, it's customary for the members of the losing boat to give their shirts to their victorious opponents. For a beer game, we think that's stretching it a bit, but the losers at least should buy the winners the next round.

Played often enough with large quantities of swill, **Boat Racing** is affectionately called — you guessed it — *"Boot Racing."*

"Better belly burst than good drink lost."
— John Ray (1670)

13.
Beer Shooting

Boot Factor: 2

Beer shooting is not really a game. Rather, it is a style of drinking beer. Quickly. It is also used to demonstrate machismo. Like the peacock's feathers, the deer's antlers, or the girth of a guy's hooter, the ability to shoot a beer, to some, demonstrates virility.

An unopened can of brew is held upside-down and punctured with a can-opener as near to the bottom of the can as possible. The "shooter" places his mouth over the hole and sucks as much air and beer into his mouth as he can. This creates a significant negative pressure in the can — visible as it dents inward. He then turns the can rightside-up and "pops" open the top. The beer literally explodes into the player's mouth, sometimes faster than he can swallow.

The combination of the cold, high-velocity beer stream and the stinging carbonation overwhelms most beginners. It is only the seasoned "shooter" who can inhale a beer properly without drooling or snarfing. A sonic belch following the shoot is key.

14.
Fuzzy Duck

Boot Factor: 2

Fuzzy Duck is a game of oral dexterity, and even fast-talking pre-law types will have a tough time with this one.

Participants assemble in a circle, and the first player begins this verbal tag game by looking at the person on his right and saying, "fuzzy duck." This second player now looks to his right and also says, "fuzzy duck." This continues around the circle until someone decides to reverse the direction of the game. To do this, a player must look at the person who just gave him the "fuzzy duck" (on his left) and say, "duzzy." This not only sends the game in the opposite direction, but also changes the passing word from "fuzzy duck" to "ducky fuzz."

The game continues in this new direction with each player looking to his left and saying "ducky fuzz" until another player says "duzzy," reversing the direction *again* and changing the passing word back to "fuzzy duck." The turkey who gets tongue-tied or breaks the tempo must drink and start the new round.

Even fledglings will realize that "fuzzy duck" and "ducky fuzz" can be twisted into obscene phrases, making **Fuzzy Duck** especially fun to play with unsuspecting parents, priests, or professors.

15.
Beer Softball

Boot Factor: 2

Beer Softball is linked to our national heritage. In the spirit of the Constitution, it introduces a system of checks and balances to ordinary softball: the more you get on base, the more you drink. Unbalanced superiority is thereby held in check by corresponding amounts of brew.

Since **Beer Softball** has been around so long, there are many variations. The classic version requires that all base-runners consume some portion of a beer, usually half a cup, before passing any base.

There are several difficulties involved with this. First, making sure all those beers are ready for consumption at each base can be a logistical nightmare. Players do best to elect a Beer Bimbo — usually someone's little brother or sister — who will faithfully serve the bases. Second, the game can proceed quite slowly, especially when sluggish drinkers find their way into the festivities. Third, after a couple of home-run balls from the hot batters, replacements for these wounded will be needed. Babe Ruth would have been a lot pudgier if he had played in this league.

Our favorite version is a little more convenient (and survivable). A keg is placed just behind second base and all base-runners must finish a whole cup before passing. The second baseman and the shortstop make sure that there are always plenty of cups filled.

16.
Categories

Boot Factor: 2

Categories is perfect if you are trying to fit in a quick beer game between classes or during a coffee break at work.

Someone starts by naming a "category," which can be anything — brands of European beer, Heismann Trophy winners, easy freshmen, whatever. One by one, players must name something in that category. The first person who fails to come up with an original addition to the category in a reasonable time must drink.

The game is great for trivia buffs. You might consider passing on a round if your opponent comes up with categories like "Uruguayan Rock Stars" or "Scenic Spots in New Jersey."

Ten Expressions For, uh, Getting Sick

1. barf
2. lose your lunch
3. wretch
4. blow chunks
5. ralph
6. technicolor yawn
7. boot
8. woof
9. reverse drink
10. liquidate your assets

17.

Beergammon

Boot Factor: 2

Though few would disagree that backgammon is one of the best board games ever invented, even fewer realize that it can be greatly improved with a simple addition: beer. No, even man's oldest board game isn't sacred.

To play **Beergammon**, play a normal game of backgammon using the doubling cube. When the game is over, the loser must drink one-quarter of a beer for every point lost.

For example, if the game was a double game, the loser drinks half a beer. No problem. But if the game was 8, 16, or 32 points, the consequences can be frightening. A 64-point game and it's all over.

To add another twist, **Beergammon** can be played so that every time a player's piece is hit and sent to the bar, he must chug half a beer. So, not only is a defeated player penalized for losing the game, he also suffers *during* the game as well. To make matters worse still, some **Beergammon** fans play for up to $1.00 a point, on top of the suds. Now you can lose your shirt as well as your lunch.

Ten More Expressions For Getting Sick

1. negative chug
2. disgorge
3. laugh at the carpet
4. shout at your shoes
5. blow lunch
6. blow doughnuts
7. blow groceries
8. blow chow
9. power boot
10. regurgitate

18.
Beer Checkers

Boot Factor: 2

Beer Checkers is not intended for old men on park benches. Rather, mixing beer and checkers makes the most boring game on earth really come to life.

To play, merely substitute Dixie cups or shot glasses filled with beer for the checkers. When your cup is jumped, you drink it. And when your men make it across the board, instead of "kinging" them and making them double shots, you can replace the beer with a shot of hard booze.

Opposing players should use different colors or styles of shot glasses. Or, better yet, use light and dark beer.

Son Of Ten Expressions For Getting Sick

1. yuke
2. earl
3. drive the porcelain bus
4. boot camp
5. heave
6. puke
7. buick
8. pray to the porcelain gods
9. toss your tacos
10. toss your cookies
11. blow foam
12. up-chuck
13. spew
14. chunder
15. talk to Ralph on the big white telephone

19.
Pookie

Boot Factor: 2

One of the world's underrated spectator sports is **Pookie**. To play, a beer gamer stands about six inches from a wall, tosses either a golf ball or a Ping-Pong ball into the air close to the wall, and tries to pin it to the wall with his forehead.

If a player misses, he will smash his face into the wall. Fun, right?

Obviously **Pookie** is a game developed for the flat-faced football set, but even the perfect preppie profile can be an advantage. An upturned prep nose is well-suited for the most demanding maneuver in **Pookie** — the Nose Ball. This feat requires the player to throw the ball up and, instead of pinning it, flip or knock it up again with his nose. He then pins it in the usual manner.

The rules for **Pookie** resemble those for Quarters. A player successfully pinning the ball decides who must drink and then goes again. A successful Nose Ball forces everyone to chug.

Players may risk a "double" — if they do not pin their first throw, they can toss again. If they miss a second time, they must drink, and the next player throws.

A few words on strategy: do not play with glasses on, do not play with a concussion, do not play against brick walls, and do not play sober. Golf balls hurt and leave red welts on the forehead and face. Ping-Pong balls are preferable but can collapse during a pin, resulting in a penalty drink for destroying equipment. And only wimps play with Nerf® balls.

The combination of a headache and a hangover, characteristic of the morning after a **Pookie** tournament, is unique. If it lasts more than a week, or if you have the urge to play again, see a doctor. You need your head examined.

Beer Finishing School

Or,

Some Great Tricks To Pull at the Party

Try as he may, a beer drinker will never be accepted by his peers until he is well-versed in the beer drinking graces. Naturally, he must know his beer and his beer games, but this is not enough. Refining certain drinking skills is simply *de rigueur*. These skills vary from silly tricks to impressive displays of drinking prowess. Knowing how to perform them distinguishes the cultured imbiber from the merely crude swiller.

Can Crushing is a skill which provides a laugh as well as a chance to display beer drinking machismo. The side of an empty aluminum beer can is dented slightly, placed against the head, and squashed into the skull. Made famous by the late John Belushi in the classic, *Animal House*.

Bottle Cap Flipping. By hooking a bottle cap over the thumb and snapping the middle finger across it, you can turn a bottle cap into a deadly projectile. The virtuoso is ambidextrous and can flip caps behind his back, between his legs, and over his head in rapid succession.

Bottle Foaming is one of the greatest party tricks and is sure to draw either a chuckle or a punch in the teeth. Tap the bottom of your beer bottle squarely on the mouth of a fellow party-goer's bottle — the more full his beer, the better — and watch masses of foam flow from his beer and flood over his hand and onto the floor.

Can Biting is on the verge of extinction, unfortunately. Yet, there is no other skill that better suggests an intimate relationship between drinker and beer. The drinker shakes an aluminum can and then bites into its side and drinks the beer as it sprays out wildly. He then tears the empty can to pieces with his teeth.

Opening Bottles With Your Teeth is an awe-inspiring skill which woos chicks and humbles guys. It is extremely useful at beach parties or on camping trips when a real bottle opener is forgotten. This practical ability can gain you instant notoriety as well as an outrageous orthodontist's bill.

Reverse Handed Drinking is a drinking technique which appears difficult but is actually a piece of cake. Before you pick up your beer, rotate your hand 180 degrees towards you. Then grab the brew and drink. Friends will envy your drinking dexterity. If you rotate after grabbing the beer, you will look really spastic.

Ear Drinking is a sleight-of-hand which leaves drunk spectators incredulous. A half-filled beer is used to fake pouring beer into an ear while at the same time beer secretly held in the mouth is allowed to drain into another cup. For most, such a feat is just a clever trick. But for those with some empty rooms upstairs, it may actually be possible.

Nose Drinking has its greatest effect when you are wearing a coat and tie and are carrying on a very serious conversation about investments, politics, or other such mature business. Nonchalantly hoist the beer to your nose, tilt your head back, and swallow. Continue your conversation as if you had just done the most natural thing in the world.

Upside-down Drinking, or drinking while standing on the head, is an activity which has come into vogue with the widespread use of gravity boots. Not only does it enliven the tedious practice of imitating a bat, but it is the most efficient use of beer, as alcohol seeks the lowest level and thus rushes right to the brain after drinking. Or something like that.

Waterfall Pouring not only looks impressive but is a way of drinking continuously, without stopping to change or refill cups. Start drinking from a cup, and pour beer into it as you drink. For even more fun, let friends join in and pour their beer into your cup, too.

Bottle Bombing is a great outlet for many frustrations. Fill a beer bottle (long-necks are preferable) with water up to an inch below the top and vigorously strike the mouth of the bottle with the flat of the palm. The bottle's bottom half will explode off with a satisfying "whommmmpft" and a crash of glass.

Draaling Beer is the finishing touch for the truly skilled beer drinker. It is a Norwegian practice in which the drinker places a bottle of beer to his lips and swings it in a circular motion. This elephantine maneuver causes the beer to swirl inside the bottle and shoot out rapidly without glugging as the drinker tilts his head back.

Pouring Beer on Your Head requires little dexterity and even less intelligence. It is, however, good for a laugh and is a great thing to do just before passing out. This moronic practice also leaves your hair shiny, clean, and manageable.

The Beer Years

When we say that beer drinking is on the rise, we aren't just blowing foam. The heartening evidence in the graph below proves that beer drinking is becoming more popular every year. Just think, while our grandparents were drinking only two and a half beers apiece per week in the late 1930's, we are consuming over five. And when this figure is adjusted for people over age 21, it almost doubles!

So, in an effort to cash in and be the first to "name" the 1980s (you know, like *The Gay Nineties*, *The Roaring Twenties*, and Tom Wolfe's *The Me Decade* of the 1970's) we suggest simply *The Beer Years*.

Okay? Does everyone agree? Is it official? Good, now where do we pick up our check?

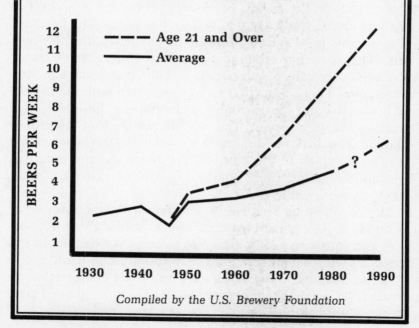

Compiled by the U.S. Brewery Foundation

The Road Trip

"Road trip." It's a phrase that evokes images of beer, camaraderie, and loose women. Anything that involves all this great stuff is naturally a rite of passage for any red-blooded college male.

Those who have never "road-tripped" may wonder what all the big fuss is about. Well, we invite all skeptics to travel with us as we recount our last great voyage and show that it is essential to the college experience.

It was a really boring night on campus. The only activities were a wine and cheese reception at the art gallery, a sing-along jamboree, and a Fellini film. Clearly, no one with any sense would dare be seen within a hundred yards of all three. There was only one option: a Road Trip!

Naturally, we were all very excited about the possibilities that lay ahead, but we had to make a few plans. The first task was to draw lots to see who would be the driver for the whole trip. This is perhaps the most tense moment of the journey, since the poor driver is absolutely forbidden to touch one drop of alcohol. This means that he has to put up with the hijinks of his loose comrades, which are always less-than-hysterical to someone who's sober. The next job was to find the proper vehicle. The dirtier and more beat-up the car, the better suited it is to the spirit of the journey. But there's also a practical reason for getting a real bomb: if a nice car is used, it's not likely to return that way.

The car must be hopelessly undersized for the number of occupants. As a general rule, compacts hold eight to ten people, and station wagons fifteen to twenty. We had about ten guys, so we tracked down a fairly shoddy compact.

Before leaving, most of us took half-hour Power Naps to insure that we'd have that extra bit of energy we'd need later to say stupid things like "So, what's your major?"

After the naps, we motivated and wedged ourselves into the car. Even though we weren't planning on returning until the following morning, no one was permitted to bring any luggage. Suitcases would only ruin the spontaneity and the adventure. Oh, except toothbrushes. Those are okay.

The first stop was just around the corner at a package store, where we bought a couple of cases of roadies for the passengers. Also known as *road pops, road sauce,* and *tweeners,* roadies are key to any road trip. Mainly, they serve to boost the road tripper's ego to staggering proportions. Upon our arrival, we had to believe that we would command the undying attention of at least 15 women. The roadies also encourage the ritualistic pit stop at the side of the highway. After all, beer can be borrowed from Mother Nature only for so long.

(This pit stop is the only stop allowed on a true road trip; the car is not permitted to even slow down to dispense the empties. For this task, experienced road trippers appoint a "bombardier" — usually the person located next to a window or under the sun roof. The bombardier is charged with tossing empties accurately at road signs, obnoxious dogs, and igneous rock formations.)

Thus assured, we went rocketing off into the night like an unguided libido. About 10 miles down the road we realized that we hadn't decided exactly where we were going. Actually, this decision wasn't all that important — many road trippers don't know where they are when they get there. All they know is they've just finished off their roadies and they must seek the nearest keg party, any keg party. And women, any women.

At last, after an hour or so, we arrived at our Valhalla, the land of beer and honeys: a sorority mixer at Mt. Smithollins College. We eagerly attacked the kegs and scoped-out the general scene. Not great, but definitely some talent. We started to work our way through the possibilities — a little small talk here, a little dancing there — to see if any women wanted to "buy some tickets to Boomtown." Not much response. We are informed that guys are "only interested in one thing." So? Explaining that it was our hormonal obligation didn't seem to help much, either.

After a few hours cuddling the keg a little and striking out a lot, we decided it was a lost cause and maybe we should rally the troops and head home that night. Unfortunately, our driver had disappeared. It seems that he was the only one sober enough to pick-up a girl and now was no where in sight.

Undaunted, we settled down on nearby couches and under convenient pianos and began concocting orgiastic stories to tell our lightweight roommates who stayed behind. After all, they missed something special.

Twenty Ways To Say "Drink"

1. pound
2. quaff
3. suck
4. shoot
5. polish off
6. do a 12-ounce curl
7. imbibe
8. potate
9. guzzle
10. chug
11. flush
12. drain
13. swig
14. inhale
15. chow bev
16. tipple
17. nurse
18. toss
19. gulp
20. bend the elbow

Boot Factor Three

Penalties in Boot Factor Three games are generally no more stringent than those in Boot Factor Two. However, since they require more mental and physical agility, Boot Factor Three games are more difficult to play. At this level, players tend to falter more often and therefore drink with greater frequency. But violent heaves are still uncommon, although players will sometimes opt for the self-induced boot in order to mollify the next morning's hangover.

Beer Golf
Whales Tails
Bullshit
Frisbeer
Dunk the Duchess
Swim Relays
Mexican
Quarters
Cups
I Never
Zoom, Schwartz, Perfigliano
Fizz Buzz
Cardinal Puff

20.
Beer Golf

Boot Factor: 3

Some people play golf sober. Really.

We don't. Ever. Neither should you.

Beer Golf differs from sober golf in one respect: linksters may deduct one stroke for every beer they manage to consume during a round (a round usually consists of only nine holes — even Jack and Arnie have problems with eighteen).

Most beer golfers down about a frostie per hole and then chug several on the final fairway. Those choosing a more ambitious pace discover the Principle of Diminishing Returns. Many also discover the meaning of octuple bogey.

Beer Golf is usually played in the form of a fraternity or club outing, which brings to light some of the sport's disadvantages. First, participants must actually plan ahead, a concept completely alien to most beer game ideology. Second, **Beer Golf** can rarely be played twice at the same course — with the management's permission, that is. It seems that greenskeepers are not partial to golf carts sunk in water hazards, 9-irons used as putters, or fairways littered with empties.

21.
Whales Tails

Boot Factor: 3

Whales Tails may very well make you an endangered species. This fast-paced game will challenge anyone's ability to stay afloat.

One person begins by chanting: "Whales Tails, Prince of Wales, Prince in the Court of (number) calls (number)." The first number is the total number of players, including the speaker. The second number designates a player that many places to the *left* of the speaker.

So if the speaker calls "five," he passes "it" to the person five places to his left around the circle. This person becomes the Prince and responds, "Nay," and the speaker then asks, "Who?" The Prince responds by calling another number, which represents the number of places to *his* left that "it" is passed.

The game continues in this way until a mistake is made or the tempo is broken. When this happens, the person responsible must drink. This game is much harder than it may seem, because each player's distance from the Prince changes every few moments as new Princes ascend the throne.

To increase the game's difficulty, the speaker may call a number higher than the total number playing. Thus, if ten are playing and the speaker calls "thirteen," then "it" goes once around the circle and ends up three places to the speaker's left. The speaker may also call his own number (equal to the number of people playing), which allows him to go again.

If everyone begins to catch on, places can be switched every few rounds. Better yet, "reversals" can be introduced to the game. For instance, whenever a multiple of two is called, the game travels in the opposite direction. Such permutations — in a game that already requires far too much thought and attention for beer-sodden players — is guaranteed to get everyone hammered.

22.
Bullshit

Boot Factor: 3

Bullshit is one of the beer games that expands the realm of human knowledge, focusing on oft-overlooked aspects of animal physiology. **Bullshit** needs no accessories, so it can be played readily anywhere or anytime. But considering its ribald content, we suggest that you avoid playing at the ballet or at funerals.

The game begins with the Master of Ceremonies asking each player in turn what brand of animal, uh, feces he wishes to be. For instance, a player can choose "horseshit," "dogshit," or even "squidshit." The emcee initiates the round by saying, "Somebody shit in the parlor." All players respond in unison, "Who shit?" The emcee blames one of the players: "Dogshit," for example. Being accused, Dogshit must reply, "Bullshit!" (as in, "Bullshit, I did not!"). The emcee asks, "Who shit?" and Dogshit responds with one of the other names, say, "Catshit." Thus the game continues, with Catshit saying "Bullshit!" and Dogshit responding "Who shit?" and Catshit blaming someone else.

This goes on until someone breaks the rhythm or responds out of turn or incorrectly. Then, naturally, he drinks. This drinker is the new Master of Ceremonies and must initiate the new round.

Here are some of the more interesting types of shit that we have encountered: swan, ewe, worm, eel, seagull, mouse, toad, pigeon, tapeworm, frog, iguana, camel, aardvark, goose, pterodactyl, bat, amoeba, Mr. Ed, Bambi, and tse-tse fly.

Of course, any type of shit that pops out is just fine. It should also be noted that the two best shits are probably "eweshit" (sounds like "you-shit" or "who-shit") and "bullshit." Both are legal and make the game even more confusing.

After a number of rounds have been played and everyone

has become accustomed to the assigned names, it is time to change identities. Better yet, the names should be changed *before* they become too familiar. This keeps people on their toes and drinking. It is also legal to introduce non-animal "shits." For example, try: eatshit, softshit, I-shit, you-shit, he-shit, we-shit, and shit-shit.

Eight Foreign Terms For "Hangover"

1. *katzenjammer* (German for "the wailing of cats")
2. *stonato* (Italian for "out of tune")
3. *la gueule de bois* (French for "woody snout")
4. *resaca* (Spanish for "surf of the sea")
5. *jeg har tommermann* (Norwegian for "workmen in my head")
6. *ont i haret* (Swedish for "pain in the roots of my hair")
7. *irie Rasta coco ganja* (Jamaican for "stoned Rastafarian trying to split my coconut")
8. *so to gi ko-ho!* (Vietnamese for "water buffalo plowing inside my head")

23.
Frisbeer

Boot Factor: 3

In an effort to distribute more equitably the destruction of brain cells, we needed a game to appeal to the mellow, "cooler-than-thou" types, as well as the fraternity/beach crowd. So, we invented **Frisbeer**, and we take full blame.

One hot summer day we were lounging around the beach, casually tossing that apotheosized disk of plastic, the Frisbee. Agreeing that we were burning up far too many calories with all that running around, we decided to bring beer into the picture. **Frisbeer** was born.

Frisbeer has little structure, so the type of people who normally throw a lot of Frisbees around will take right to it. Two players start about 30 or 40 yards apart and place a bottle or can of beer in front of them. The players then take turns throwing a Frisbee at each other's beers. If your beer is hit, you must take a healthy gulp. After a hit, the player who just drank must take one pace toward his opponent. This continues until the players are right on top of each other, making for some pretty rapid suds-sucking.

Once next to each other, players continue to pace in *opposite* directions until they are again about 30 or 40 yards apart. At this point, the players begin to walk toward each other again. This process can continue, well, as long as you feel like it.

If there are more than two players, participants should start by forming a geometric shape, with one competitor at each vertex (an equilateral triangle for three, a square for four, a dodecagon for twelve, etc.). Each player throws to his right. If a player's beer is hit, he takes a pace toward the player who just threw. Players will begin to spiral toward the center point and then spiral outward again. Such cosmic configurations often prove astonishing to those partaking in substances less legal than beer. Oh, wow.

24.
Dunk the Duchess

Boot Factor: 3

Dunk the Duchess lets you play submarine commander —
coolly, coldly calculating the best way to submerge your opponent. We learned **Dunk the Duchess** on a foray to a dive
Irish bar on Manhattan's West Side. We had so much fun that
we finished nine pitchers before the bartender decided it was
time for us to leave.

To begin, players need two full pitchers and one glass per
person, plus one extra glass. Float the extra glass in one of
the pitchers. The lip of the glass should protrude about an
inch or so above the surface of the beer. (Depending on the
type of glass used, a little beer may need to be poured into
the glass to steady it.) A narrow, pilsner-style glass that tapers
toward the bottom has the best buoyancy characteristics.

Players then fill their glasses from the second pitcher and
take turns pouring beer into the floating glass. Each player
is responsible for the glass for five seconds (counted aloud)
after he pours. After the five count, the glass is the respon-
sibility of the next player. The perfect pour is one that causes
the glass to sink after five and half seconds, thereby screw-
ing the next player before he has time to pour. The player
who sinks the glass to the bottom of the pitcher must retrieve
it and relieve it of its new-found contents.

Near the end of a round, as the glass actually floats *below*
surface level (due to surface tension), skillful drop-by-drop
pours become crucial. It is illegal to steady your hand by
resting the pouring cup on the edge of the pitcher.

Dunk the Duchess gets very messy, and we recommend
that you keep several Mung Rags on hand.

25.
Swim Relays

Boot Factor: 3

Swim Relays, like ducks, can only be found in Florida during the winter. To participate, you must head south, say to Fort Lauderdale, during Spring Break.

The race is staged at bars or hotels that have pools and is usually held right before the wet t-shirt contest (which is what people have really come to see). Teams are formed along college or fraternity lines. At the gun, the first swimmer for each team chugs a full beer and then swims the length of the pool. The second swimmer then chugs his beer and swims back, and so on until one team wins.

We suggest you do not try this at home unless your pool has a very good filter system. The "aqua boot" is not a pretty sight.

Fifteen Ways To Say "Drunk"

1. soused
2. plastered
3. corked
4. lit-up
5. scuppered
6. bent out of shape
7. faced
8. squashed
9. trashed
10. wiped-out
11. plowed
12. swamped
13. blasted
14. reeling
15. muddled

26.
Mexican

Boot Factor: 3

In most beer games, a modicum of practice and skill can keep a player from drinking too much and blowing his groceries. But in **Mexican**, the gaming *hombre* is at the mercy of the dice. Whether he tosses his tacos and takes an unscheduled siesta depends little on his training for the game. A few unlucky rolls, a few unsuccessful bluffs, and the beer will mount faster than the Third World debt.

The object of **Mexican** is to be the last player in the game. It begins with each player placing a die, known as the "scoring die," on the table in front of him, with the six showing. The first player shakes two "game dice" in a cup and turns the cup upside-down on the table so that his roll is hidden from view. He peeks and recovers the dice.

A roll of 1:2 is called a "Mexican" and is the best possible roll. The best other rolls, in decreasing value, are as follows: 6:6, 5:5, 4:4, 3:3, 2:2, 1:1, and then 6:5, 6:4, 6:3, 6:2, 6:1, 5:4, 5:3, 5:2, 5:1, 4:3, 4:2, 4:1, 3:2, 3:1.

After assessing his roll, the player turns to his left and either admits his roll or bluffs. The second player may then do one of two things:

1) He can choose to believe the first player's call. If he does, he must re-roll the game dice to try to beat the first player's roll.

2) He may accuse the first player of bluffing by saying, "You're bluffing," "No way, bud," "Eat me," etc. The accused then must uncover his roll.

If the first player was indeed bluffing, the point goes to the challenger. Otherwise, the point goes to the accused.

In either case, the loser of a point receives a stiff penalty — generally half a cup or more — and must then turn his scoring die from 6 to 5. The game continues around the table, with the defeated player of each round consuming brew and then turning his scoring die down one.

When a player with a 1 showing on his scoring die loses a point, he must drink a larger than normal penalty and then leave the game. The game ends when only one player remains.

Fifteen More Ways To Say "Drunk"

1. boxed
2. wasted
3. basted
4. hammered
5. shellacked
6. stinko
7. blitzed
8. gassed
9. primed
10. skunked
11. slaughtered
12. stiff
13. gooned
14. gone Borneo
15. smashed

27.
Quarters

Boot Factor: 3

Without a doubt, **Quarters** is the most popular drinking game in America. The game's popularity stems from its mobility and its exciting mix of chance, skill, revenge, and serious power drinking. Above all, the opportunity to make an opponent grovel at your feet simply because you can plunk a quarter into a cup of beer 10, 20, even 30 consecutive times gives endless gratification to sadistic pleasure-seekers.

The quintessential **Quarters** table is six-inch-thick Honduran mahogony smoothed to a fine finish with multiple coats of varnish. Of course, any bar table will suffice. The game begins with a beer-filled cup placed on the table in front of one person, who tries to bounce a quarter off the table so that it lands in the cup. If successful, the thrower gets to make *any* player drink all the beer in the cup. He then re-throws.

If the quarter ever hits the rim, the thrower gets to re-toss. If he hits three rims in a row, however, he must drink the beer in the cup. When the thrower misses the cup completely, he must pass the cup to the next player, or he can call a "double." A "double" allows him to throw again. If he misses or hits the rim on the "double" throw, he drinks. If he sinks the quarter, he can make any opponent chug, but the thrower cannot toss again, and he passes the cup and the quarter.

Suicide Quarters, a more intense version for real sickos, is played similarly, except that an extra cup of beer is placed directly behind the first cup. If the quarter bounces too far and lands in the second cup, the thrower must drink *both* cups. All the other rules are the same as one cup **Quarters**. A rim shot on the second cup also means a re-throw. If the thrower hits three rims in a row on either cup, he drinks only one cup.

Quarters can and should be practiced anywhere, at anytime. Give up twiddling your thumbs, biting your nails, and spanking your monkey, and dedicate that precious time to bouncing your quarter. Throwing consistently is truly an art; the motion must become ingrained, second nature, even genetic. One tossing technique is to hit the edge of the quarter on the table. Another is to hit the flat face off the surface. Most prefer the latter, since it gives more control.

Besides throwing a quarter, rifling down a brew with a quarter resting on the bottom lends another element of challenge to the game. The beer is properly polished-off only when the drinker holds the empty cup in one hand and displays the quarter clenched between his front teeth. There is, however, a direct correlation between degree of inebriation and frequency of quarter munching. Many a neophyte player has exclaimed after drinking, "You mean there was a quarter in this cup?!" The x-rays are a side-splitter.

Above all, **Quarters** is a game of attack and revenge, screw and be screwed. A player gloating over a string of 15 consecutive sinks deserves to be punished. Heavily.

Son Of Fifteen Ways To Say "Drunk"

1. bombed
2. buzzed
3. pickled
4. gagged
5. soaked
6. brained
7. whalloped
8. grogged
9. pissed
10. stoked
11. stained
12. twisted
13. shit-faced
14. wracked
15. steamed

28.
Cups

Boot Factor: 3

Cups is perfect for bars and frugal beer gamers who don't want to invest in equipment. All you need are beer and plastic cups.

The object of **Cups** is to flip your cup in the air at least one full revolution so that it lands standing-up on either end. If a player flips the cup and it lands right-side up, the next player in rotation must finish a whole cup of beer. If the cup lands upside-down, the next player must drink just half a beer. If the cup lands on its side, the "flipper" must take a healthy sip of his beer. And if the cup rolls off the table, the flipper must drink a whole beer. After each flip, regardless of the outcome, the cup is passed.

When a cup lands on one of its ends, the player who must drink can decide to reverse the direction of the game simply by saying so before he flips his cup. The game travels in the new direction until another player reverses. The beauty of this rule is that it allows for head to head battles between neighboring players.

This game was originally developed to familiarize beer drinkers with their most important tool, the cup. **Cups** was unheard of in ancient times (i.e., before the invention of fast food), when man drank only from bottles and cans. The advent of the keg party spawned the cup subculture that has been growing steadily since the 1950's.

An interesting variation of **Cups** is **Cans**. In this contest, players flip a full can until it lands upright. When that happens, the next player in rotation must open the well-shaken can under his nose and then drink it. If the can rolls off the table or lands on its side, penalty drinks are taken from the flipper's own cup.

29.

I Never

Boot Factor: 3

I Never is a drinking version of the old games "20 Questions" and "Truth or Dare." Once you start playing, you may swear you'll never play again.

One person starts the game by making an "I Never" statement like "I never have been drunk," whether it's true or not. Each player who cannot truthfully agree with this "I Never" statement must drink. (In this case, whoever has been drunk, must drink.) If everyone playing can honestly agree with the "I Never" just stated, then the player who offered the statement must drink.

Now, all this sounds pretty silly — until you imagine playing with a group of people who don't know each other very well. All you have to do is make some outlandish "I Never" statement like "I never have had sex with anyone in this group" and then wait to see who drinks. The potential for abuse is unlimited.

Return Of Fifteen Ways To Say "Drunk"

1. loaded	9. blotto
2. looped	10. bagged
3. out of control	11. tanked
4. slozzled	12. pie-eyed
5. ripped	13. paralytic
6. toasted	14. sauced
7. skewered	15. sopped
8. juiced	

30.
Zoom, Schwartz, Perfigliano

Boot Factor: 3

Zoom, Schwartz, Perfigliano is the word-game of choice for neophyte gamesters and experts alike. Z.S.P. is a verbal tag game whose rules are easily understood in theory, but nearly impossible to apply in practice.

One player begins with these exact words: "The name of the game is 'Zoom, Schwartz, Perfigliano'." At this point, the speaker is "it." The point is to keep passing "it" to other players without blundering.

At first, the only three commands are *Zoom*, *Schwartz*, and *Perfigliano*. To start, the speaker looks at another player and says, "Zoom." The player at whom the speaker was looking is now "it," and has three options:

1) He can look at any player except the person who just gave "it" to him and say, "Zoom." That player now is "it" and continues the game. You cannot "zoom" the person who just gave "it" to you.

2) He can look right back at the person who just gave "it" to him and say, "Schwartz." This gives "it" back to this player.

3) He can look at any player except the person who just gave him "it" and say, "Perfigliano." This also gives "it" right back to the first player.

The game continues with each new "it" passing "it" along according to these rules. Of course, as the game's tempo increases, **Z.S.P.** becomes very confusing, and everyone gets pretty pie-eyed. Note that direct eye contact with the person to whom a player is speaking is crucial; roving eyes indicate unfamiliarity with the rules and earn the clueless sap a drink. An improper introduction (words deleted, rearranged, or added) also means a penalty. The loser drinks and restarts the game until he gets it right.

Once three-word **Z.S.P.** has been mastered, additional titles should be introduced. They are usually added one at a time in the following order: *Butaman, Coleman, Smith, Uncle Toby?*, and *Morowitz*. When the players have decided to add a new name, they must include it in their introduction from then on. For example, "The name of the game is *Zoom, Schwartz, Perfigliano, Butaman, Coleman*, etc." The new additions do the following:

Butaman gives "it" to the player on the immediate right of the speaker — regardless of whom the speaker is looking at when he says "Butaman."

Coleman gives "it" to the player on the immediate left of whomever the speaker is looking at when he says "Coleman."

Smith gives "it" to whoever says "Smith." In effect, a "Smith" does nothing, but it can be used to stall or bait newcomers.

Uncle Toby? gives "it" to the player two places to the right of whomever the speaker is looking at when he says "Uncle Toby?" However, before the new "it" can continue the game, the person at whom the speaker was looking when he said "Uncle Toby?" must respond "yes" in a low, drawn, Lurch-like voice — "yeeeeesss." This person then does nothing, and the player two places to his right continues the game.

Morowitz transfers "it" to the player who spoke two turns before the "Morowitz" was used. For advanced players only.

Of course, these commands may be included or deleted on a whim. And it is perfectly legal and quite humorous to make up new titles. As the night rolls on, titles like *Lovelace* are added and provoke all the requisite sound effects, like choking.

Zoom, Schwartz, Perfigliano looks pretty ridiculous on paper, but it is definitely worth the effort to learn.

31.
Fizz Buzz

Boot Factor: 3

If there were ever a game to initiate, infatuate, and intoxicate players of all ages, **Fizz Buzz** is it. Though players need no mathematical genius to succeed — we've played with math majors who couldn't get anywhere — played regularly, **Fizz Buzz** should bring up standardized test scores at least ten percentile points.

Fizz Buzz is a counting game in which the players try to reach higher levels of success on each round. The gist is this: when a player reaches a number that has a 5 in it (e.g., 5, 15, 25, 50, etc.) or is a multiple of 5 (5, 10, 15, 20, etc.) he says "fizz" instead of the number. If a number has a 7 (7, 17, 27, 70, etc.) or is a multiple thereof (7, 14, 21, etc.), he says "buzz." The apparent simplicity is deceptive.

One player starts by stating a number between 1 and 4 and saying "to my right" or "to my left" to indicate whether the player on his right or left continues. The next player then adds 1 to the number, and so on. The game continues in this way with each player adding 1 and saying "fizz" or "buzz" when appropriate. Whenever anyone says "buzz," however, the direction in which the game is travelling *reverses*.

Players will eventually realize that some numbers are multiples of both 5 and 7 and/or include both 5 and 7, or two 5's or two 7's for that matter. A number can only get one of the following designations: "fizz," "buzz," "fizz-buzz," "fizz-fizz," or "buzz-buzz." We've already covered "fizz" and "buzz." The numbers that get "fizz-buzz" are 35, 57, and 75 because they are multiples of 5 and 7 and/or include 5 and 7. The numbers that get "fizz-fizz" are 15, 25, 45, 55, 65, etc. because they are multiples of 5 and include a 5. The only number worthy of the awesome, double-direction change "buzz-buzz" is 77, a multiple of and including 7.

In our zeal to recount the game, we almost forgot to say

that the player who breaks the game's tempo or says "bizz" or "fuzz" or "shit, what number is it again?" must imbibe heavily and start the game again.

As a game stretches long into the night, the practice and polishing of constant repetition is easily offset by even moderate amounts of alcohol. A group reaching 40 or 50 in the beginning of an evening is lucky to break 15 by the end.

Bride Of Fifteen Ways To Say "Drunk"

1. polluted
2. gone
3. tight
4. slambasted
5. sloshed
6. cocked
7. canned
8. fired-up
9. jacked-up
10. fubar
11. tuned-out
12. faceless
13. potted
14. crocked
15. totalled

32.
Cardinal Puff

Boot Factor: 3

Cardinal Puff is one of the oldest and best drinking games around. Unfortunately, we can't tell you the rules.

You see, the game's rules and traditions are maintained by a sacred order of members who call themselves "Cardinals." The only way to learn the game is to seek out a Cardinal — simply by asking everyone you meet "Are you a Cardinal?" — and have him pass his knowledge on to you.

If you succeed in learning the game, which entails drinking every time you make a mistake while learning the ritual, then you become a Cardinal and a keeper of the game. The members of this secret, loyal society travel by the creed, "Once a Cardinal, always a Cardinal."

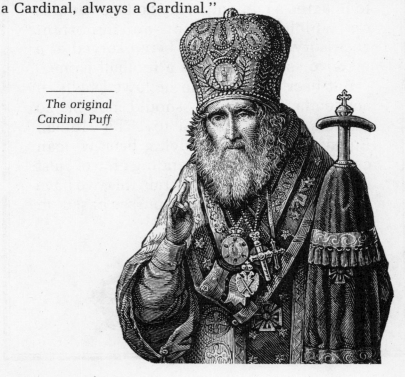

*The original
Cardinal Puff*

Introduction to
The Beer Curriculum

For better or worse, beer has always been closely associated with education. It is hard to imagine a contemporary college campus on which beer is not an important accessory, whether it is being served at a mixer or smuggled into a football game.

But beer's role in the hallowed halls of academia is not and should not be so limited. Beer is central to "The Human Equation," and by studying beer we can come to a better understanding of, well, just about everything! To illustrate this, we have developed a sampling of courses based on the subject of beer.

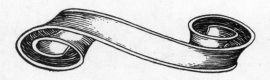

History 124:

Beer: The Catalyst of History

What serious historian could doubt that beer has been the single most important factor in the development of civilization?

It all began over 20,000 years ago with the invention of the wheel. With the wheel, man created the means to road trip to women's caves and to prehistoric package stores. The problem was that he had not yet invented beer. So for ages, civilization stagnated. Man demonstrated the intellectual prowess of Conan the Barbarian and the aesthetic appeal of a stegasaurus. Life was slow, and man was slower. The species was waiting for an evolutionary catalyst. It was waiting for beer.

Suddenly, about 4,000 years ago, the Mesopotamians, history's original party monsters, put an end to the Stone Age by brewing the earth's first swill. These great guys ruled the world single-handedly for centuries and drank lots of beer.

Then, one dark and embarrassing day, the power of the Mesopotamians was challenged by a clever group of men who drank wine and wore dresses — namely, the Greeks and Romans. These effete cads suppressed beer-drinking for a millenium. Soon, feudal wars broke out all over Europe, as people, fed up with religious oppression and overly strict Medieval Blue Laws, demanded their right to drink the golden nectar again.

Fortunately, these dark ages were eventually lightened by the Renaissance and the rebirth of sculpture, painting, and beer-gaming. Men were just beginning to learn that life was not necessarily a painful experience and that it was okay to go out and party-down once in a while without incurring the wrath of some bishop, God, or other ecclesiastical big-wig.

Then, late in the 1600's, a group of guys facetiously known as the "Puritans" decided that living on the Continent had

A Mesopotamian hieroglyphic shows the brewing techniques of history's original party monsters.

become too much like watching re-runs of Ingmar Bergman movies — everyone was discussing their "feelings" and no one wanted to just go out and get crazy. They were fed up, so the Puritans packed their toothbrushes one Friday night and decided to road-trip to the New World. Also, they had heard there were girls there.

We can safely assume that the Puritans were playing some vicious beer games during their journey on the Mayflower. After all, the captain's log is full of accounts of the passengers spending hours bent over the ship's railing, heaving into the Atlantic. After stumbling onto Massachusetts, our partying forefathers decreed that in the New World, no French would be spoken, no fern bars would be built, and beer would always be on tap. These were the humble beginnings of a truly awesome nation.

Three and a half centuries have gone by, and America has

been drinking beer and kickin' ass ever since. We're 10-and-1 in major wars! We've invented everything worth inventing, except maybe pasteurized milk. Cars, planes, light bulbs, pizza, hamburgers, the telephone, and Daytona Beach — the rest of the world owes us in a big way. And we know that they all secretly envy our crazy, beer-guzzling culture. Even France.

All in all, it seems clear that the U.S. of A. has reaffirmed the historic link between beer and world leadership.

Russia, you ask? Are you kidding? They drink vodka, for God's sake. Bad vodka at that. You might as well do shots of rubbing alcohol. Maybe if their hockey team had had a few more cold ones, they might not have looked so stupid in the 1980 Olympics.

Alas, not everything is rosy in this land of red, white, and blue. California wines have become quite popular, and daiquiri-serving fern bars have popped-up in gentrified urban areas everywhere. Should these trends continue, we could quickly lose that mental toughness that keeps us on top. Let's face it, during the Cuban Missile Crisis, President Kennedy surely pounded some brews the night before he told the commies to go screw themselves. He did not sniff Chablis.

On the other hand, *detente* was probably conceived at a wine and cheese reception at the Soviet Embassy. And look where that got us.

We study history because we can learn valuable lessons from the past and because it's usually required for graduation. The lesson here is clear: beer drinkers don't mess around when it comes to world affairs. They get right to the top, and they stay there. We've got to keep socking down those frosties if we're going to keep the world safe for democracy and great keg parties. So rally, America, rally!

Biology 450:

The Anatomy of a Hangover

Since Necessity is the mother of Invention, beer swillers have concocted some of the most elaborate, most vile, and most effective ways of dealing with that post-pleasure demon, Mr. Hangover.

But before we discuss the cures, we should consider the cause of the hangover. Simply, if you drink beer quicker than your liver can remove beer's alcohol from your blood, excess alcohol remains free to cruise around your body and wreak havoc.

You see, the liver is where the "chemistry-nerd" cells of the body gather. When alcohol reaches these pale, calculator-toting misfits, these nerds begin to perform chemistry experiments to destroy it. But competition in the liver is fierce, and each cell sabotages his neighbor's experiments and tries to be the first to break down the alcohol and look good to the Professor cell. But the Profesor cell isn't helping them with their assignment, so it can take these cells over an hour to destroy the alcohol from just one beer.

So if you drink more than one beer an hour, you'll have some excess alcohol, which has time to travel all over your body and do major damage to your cells. It destroys electrolytes, precious bodily fluids, and the eight essential vitamins and iron you got from your breakfast cereal. In addition, the alcohol will wage guerrilla warfare on Mission Control — your brain. Your brain cells will be forced to surrender one by one, lobe by lobe, until all but a few vital brain centers remain functioning: those controlling heartbeat, respiration, copius urination, and the strong desire for food and sex. Thus, alcohol not only trashes the chemicals in your body, it also makes you act silly, eat too much, drink too much, and stay up too late. And of course, none of this helps much the morning after.

So when you wake up, you are parched, your body and head ache from chemical imbalances, and you quiver, sway, and have trouble talking because your electrolytes are all screwed-up.

What can the drinker do to soften the blow? Well, we've found three opportune times to attend to hangovers: before drinking, before bed, and before waking up. Each has its merits and drawbacks, as shown below:

Before drinking: Remedial action before any alcohol even enters the bloodstream shows impressive foresight. The advantage is that you are sober enough to carry out the prescribed remedy. The disadvantage is that such preventive action is basically useless. Medical practice suggests eating a large meal of fatty and oily foods and bread, in order to line the stomach and slow the absorption of alcohol. Our practice is pizza.

Before bed: This is the most effective time to take action against the hangover. Unfortunately, you are usually too trashed to do anything but fall on your mattress. Medical practice suggests taking vitamins and minerals and drinking water. Our practice is to get some late burgers, take two aspirin, chug as many glasses of water as possible, and crash.

After waking: Ideally, you have already done enough to significantly lessen your hangover, and you feel pretty good when you awake. Realistically, you are in pain. Medical practice suggests that you lie still in a dark room, sip soda water, take some aspirin, and rest. Our practice is to chug two warm beers, throw on the Ray-Bans, go eat lunch, and get psyched to do it again.

As you can tell, there are slight discrepancies between accepted hangover remedies and our practices. Though we don't guarantee that you'll live past 35 using our methods, at least they're more fun.

Biology Lab 101:

Perfecting
The Power Chug

The art of chugging has always been shrouded in dark mystery, its secrets veiled to the uninitiated. Many non-chuggers perceive chugging as a miraculous feat of contortionism, a God-given ability, possessed by a lucky few, to inhale beer.

But these misguided sippers need not despair. Power chugging is an acquired trait, a skill to be learned, just like riding a bicycle. Once done right, the ability to power chug is never forgotten. The key to inhaling beer is the disciplined application of scientific principles, not luck.

Remember, too, that once you learn to chug, you need never drink any liquid in the traditional fashion. For years, parents and teachers have conditioned us to drink politely — to swallow only small mouthfuls of liquid at a time. Try to undo this conditioning and teach yourself to guzzle without stopping to swallow. Be prepared to practice every day if necessary, until you develop the "feel."

The best time to practice is in the shower, just before a meal so the stomach is empty. Find a suitable cup and fill it with lukewarm water. Now, get psyched: relax the mouth, throat, and chest. Breathe deeply and slowly. Chant a mantra like "want that beer, want that beer." Bring the liquid to your lips. Your head should be tilted up only slightly — if you bend too much, your esophagus will constrict. Exhale fully and pour the water steadily into your mouth, more by tilting the cup and bending backward at the waist than by tilting your head. The goal is to achieve maximum throat dilation with the passage to the lungs closed (the physiological analog to woofing, but in reverse). You may choke, sputter, and snarf the first few times, but that's because your airway is open and some water has decided to check out your lungs. The best way to develop proper technique is to imagine yourself swimming underwater in the ocean. You break through the surface and a wave crashes on your face. Suddenly you have gulped a mass of water without even trying. The liquid rifled down your throat and you didn't even swallow! This is the feeling you must recapture when you chug.

Being able to power chug has many practical applications. A position on a top Tang team is won by only the most dedicated and most talented chuggers — the *creme de la creme* of chugging, so to speak. When we interviewed for jobs and graduate schools, we were often asked our chug times. If he hadn't run out of time during the Presidential debate, Ronald Reagan was going to ask Jimmy Carter what his chug time was. It is one of those things that determines whether or not you "make the grade."

Anyway, remember that the only way to be a truly cool beer gamester is through impressive beer inhaling. But you've got to practice, practice, practice. Soon, you too will develop the "feel" and become a real beer stud.

Limbering exercises also help the beginning Power Chugger.

Music 420:

The Role of Beer In Classical Music

Classical music is a lot like filet of pig's knuckle. Both are enjoyed by small groups of esthetes trying to prove their superior taste. Take opera, for example. Who really enjoys watching a fat guy warble in a boring foreign language to some soprano who looks like Miss Piggy?

Fortunately, not all pre-rock 'n roll music can be dismissed so quickly. In fact, many old songs are filled with tales of fun folks having good times. And their enjoyment, then as now, often included some generous libations.

Our national anthem, for instance, was not always concerned with "bombs bursting in air." Francis Scott Key borrowed the tune from the theme song of a British men's club, whose members were concerned with getting bombed in a different manner. The original version of the song has nothing to do with "the home of the brave." Instead, it ends with a toast, proposing that the club should "intwine...with Bacchus's vine."

Alright, what's wrong with that quotation?

Wine, that's what. This song, rousing as it may have been, perpetuates the enduring and erroneous view that wine is more sophisticated than beer. Just as many socialites today prefer Chateaux Effete or Perrier over a good, cold Bud, so too in the past did many drinkers regard beer as a symbol of the great unwashed hordes.

Luckily, many song writers have exhibited a clearer understanding of beer's importance. Bedrich Smetana, a 19th century Czech composer, reveals such insight in his opera *The Bartered Bride*:

> *You foam within our glasses, you lusty golden brew.*
> *Whoever imbibes will take fire from you.*
> *The young and the old sing your praises.*
> *Here's to beer. Here's to cheer. Here's to beer.*

Medieval monks especially valued their beer. The pious, celibate image we have of monks just disguised the lusty truth: monasteries in the Dark Ages were equivalent to today's frat houses. The brethren may have served God, but they also served lots of brew. Johann Schein, a 16th century German composer, reveals the advanced level of drinking technique found in the monasteries. Note especially the references to proper chugging form:

> *So my fellow friars, who wants to be sad now?*
> *Sing, play! We must have good cheer.*
> *With such good beer...bottoms up.*
> *Empty it in one swift gulp.*
> *The glass must be entirely inverted.*

Great guys, eh?

A number of composers shared a common view about the place of women in drinking society. Women, they believed, should not be sober independents or mere house slaves, content to be inebriated with their love for their hubby. No, women should be good drinking buddies. This attitude is suggested in the famous aria *Back and Side Go Bare* from an opera by English composer Ralph Vaugh Williams with text by His Holiness, Bishop John Still:

> *And Tib my wife, that as her life*
> *Loveth well good ale to seek,*
> *Full oft drinks she, tell ye may see*
> *The tears run down her cheek:*

While on the subject of love, many know the tune of Bo Derek's musical aphrodisiac *Bolero*, composed by Maurice Ravel. Ravel also dealt with other, more liquid forms of fulfillment. Spurning the sophisticated, sherry-sipping, I-like-the-taste school of drinking, Ravel in his *Drinking Song* proposed a no-nonsense rationale for sucking down those beers:

> *I drink to joy*
> *Joy is the one aim*
> *to which I go straight when I am drunk.*

Ravel probably would have been good buddies with Beethoven. When ol' Ludwig Von finished a tough day of inventing new musical forms and distilling the pathos of the human experience, he liked to go down to the corner pub and lift a few with the guys. Though unable to win free games on baroque pinball machines, Beethoven reveals in his song *Come Fill* that he knew how to drink:

> Come fill, fill, my good fellow!
> Fill high, high, my good fellow!
> And let's be merry and mellow,
> And let us have one bottle more...
> Huzzah! then for one bottle more!

Though Ravel and Beethoven have not composed for some time (in fact, they are now actively decomposing), their musical love for beer thrives in many college drinking songs. *The Stein Song* of the University of Michigan is a fine example. Note the unforced lyricism of the rhyme scheme and the subtle dialectic between assonance and consonance in the final line:

> Michigan, Michigan, may your glory never pale,
> To your prosperity, we drink down our ale.
> May our sons of future years, like their dads today,
> Whooper up for Michigan, hooray, hooray, hooray!

Despite such rousing lyrics, we think the art of the drinking song reached its zenith in the 19th-century. For instance, even though *The Morning After* admits that beer can affect your system like Drano, it shows that the true drinking enthusiast always has the ability to rally:

> A heated interior, a wobbly bed,
> A sea-sick man with an aching head;
> Whiskey, beer, gin, booze galore,
> Were introduced to the cuspidor!
>
>> And with morning came bags of ice
>> So very necessary in this life of vice;
>
> And when I colled my throbbing brain,
> Did I swear off and quit?
> No, I got soused again.

In sum, we hope we have demonstrated that composers, like their brother writers and playwrights, are partiers, too. With all this evidence, it should be quite clear why everybody sings when they're trashed.

Sociology 125:
Beer: The Social Lubricant

Beer makes you, uh, horny. It also makes you drunk. This common combination can produce some interesting results, and a hangover may not be the only thing you wake up with the next morning. But worse, beer has the uncanny ability to lower your aesthetic judgement by shocking degrees. Baker's Law applies best: at 3:00 a.m. when you're really trashed, everybody looks attractive.

When sober, most people are initially attracted to those in the 7 to 10 range (i.e., good-looking members of the opposite sex). But as the beers go down, so do the aesthetic standards — precipitously, as demonstrated in the graph below:

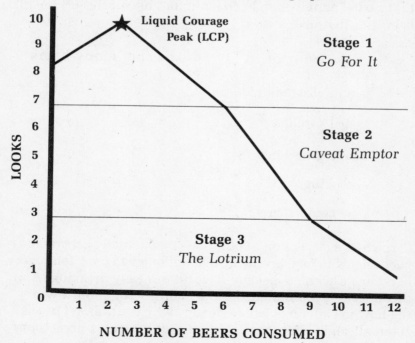

First, you enter the *Caveat Emptor* ("Let the buyer beware") stage. You enter this stage after a six-pack or so, and people normally considered plain (the 3 to 6 range) start to look pretty decent. You just have to hope that none of your friends are around to remind you otherwise next morning.

Really late in the evening, some unfortunate people pass to the dreaded *Lotrium* level. ("Lotrium" is a Bantu word meaning loosely "snorting polyester beast.") Encounters that occur at this stage are disgusting but excusable, because they are symptoms of a form of myopia affectionately known as "night blindness," which can lead to an even more distressing plight: the Coyote Morning. (The Coyote Morning occurs when you awake the next morning after a binge and discover that the person sleeping on your arm next to you is so repugnant that you would rather chew off your arm than chance waking him/her when you get up to leave.) The shock of a Coyote Morning and the risk of contracting the Big H are enough to cause even the most promiscuous hoser to think twice.

On the brighter side of such rude awakenings is the fact that sexual activity can burn a number of calories off the ol' beer gut. Just take a look:

One hour of	Burns this many beers
scoping/swooping	1
visual foreplay	3
heavy grovelling	5
skrocking	10
post-coital regret	15

You see, a case of night blindness can actually get you into good shape! In fact, one lucky night of requited concupiscence can burn a whole weekend's worth of heavy drinking. And this doesn't even include all the calories you'll burn worrying how to explain to your "steady" why you weren't in your room all night. But what the hell — it'll make a great story some day.

English 202: Non-Fiction Writing

"The Day I Entered a Fern Bar and Lived to Tell About It"

A True Story

I had stayed up all night playing Quarters and Slush Fund, and I awoke the next afternoon with a manly hangover and a stomach in desperate need of solid nutrition. So, in search of a good cheeseburger and a tall, cool Bud, I wandered aimlessly, shielding my eyes from the sunset, into some place that seemed like a decent eating establishment.

Boy, was I wrong. I was lucky to leave with my hormones intact.

Upon entering, my senses were assaulted by a deluge of brass, brick, stained glass, and hanging plants. Dismayed but still too hungover to really care, I slumped down at a table. Suddenly, a waitress materialized: "I'm sorry, sir, but you'll have to wait to be seated." As she led me back to the bar, leaves and twigs brushed menacingly against my face. I was told to wait by a well-lit tank full of tropical fish.

Trying to make the best of things, I decided to find the jukebox. "Maybe I'll crank some tunes and liven this place up," I thought. But just as soon as I began my search, a Barry Manilow song slithered from an overhead speaker. No *real* jukebox has Barry Manilow songs, I realized. A quick glance through the red and green drinks on the bar confirmed my fears. The bartender had just put ol' B.M.'s *Greatest Hits* album into a concealed tape deck.

Seven thoroughly nauseating songs later, I was taken to a table with a small candle in the middle. The table was beside a large window — large enough to insure that every passing pedestrian could watch me eat my cheeseburger. A wispy-looking waiter waltzed over and lisped, "Hi, my name is David, and I'll be your host for the evening."

Host?

"Can I get you a drink?" he continued. "You look as though you might be thirsty for a wine spritzer. Or perhaps one of our fresh fruit daiquiris?"

I still didn't fully understand where I was, but my natural instincts put me on the defensive.

"Cheeseburger. Budweiser," I said. I was not smiling.

David sauntered off and, 20 minutes later, still bored and beerless, I decided to eavesdrop on the couple at the next table. They seemed to be engaged in a serious conversation:

"Look, Mark, you're just not growing with me. You don't understand my needs. I really, like, have to explore the range of my personality."

"But, Brooke — "

"No, Mark, I need my own space, my own identity. I have to find out who I am."

"But, Brooke — "

"I'm sorry, Mark, but I'm, like, really into honesty, you know? Our relationship is just too confining."

"But, Brooke — "

I was amazed that people could spew such rot. Where was I, anyway? My hangover was subsiding, and I was finally beginning to understand my predicament when David arrived with my order. "Enjoy," he said, with a flurry of gesticulations. "If there's anything you need, just whistle."

God.

My "cheeseburger" turned out to be a bunless beef sandwich smothered in bleu cheese and sauteed mushrooms. And served in a wicker basket, no less.

My rejuvenated brain cells suddenly put the pieces of this gruesome puzzle together — hanging plants, Barry Manilow, and fernspeak — I had stumbled into a Fern Bar! I knew that if I didn't get out of there fast, the aroma of the plants would affect my powers of reason and good taste, and I'd soon be ordering Melon Balls and spinach quiche.

I chugged most of my beer, poured the rest on the candle, laid a five-spot on the table, and made a Power Dash for the door.

I stumbled onto the sidewalk and inhaled the evening air with relief. I had escaped, and, luckily, none of my friends had seen me in the window. I headed straight for Rudy's, the only place I knew that I could get a real cheeseburger. Raw.

Boot Factor Four

In Boot Factor Four games, there are only survivors. At B.F. 4, the best you can hope for is to avoid being the sap who ends up passing out or blowing cookies. Boot Factor Four survivors have applied acquired gaming skill and technique to sustain the ravages of these games. These remarkable athletes sample the bittersweet pleasure of advanced beer-gaming: the thrill of victory and the agony of a probable cleansing at the hands of the Porcelain Gods.

Beer-an-Inning
Shot-a-Minute
Yards
Caps
Acey-Deucey
Hi-Lo
Red-Black
Dimes
Beer Pong
Volley Pong
Blow Pong
Bladder Bust

Beer-an-Inning can be a lot of fun for fans and players alike.

33.

Beer-an-Inning

Boot Factor: 4

Baseball is American. Drinking beer is American. So, what could be more logical than combining baseball and beer drinking? What — besides peanuts and Cracker Jack — could complete a wholesome outing to the ol' ballpark but a hearty beer drinking game?

When we're at the diamond, we like to play **Beer-an-Inning**. The rules are simple: start every inning with a full cup of beer and finish it by the end of the inning.

A leisurely task, many assume. Don't kid yourself. Though it is acceptable to drink 12-ounce beers, it is preferable, indeed sporting, to use the 16-ounce, 20-ounce, or 24-ounce models. And since **Beer-an-Inning** is properly played at live ball games, you must drink whatever swill the stadium sells. Playing **Beer-an-Inning** to a game on television is permissable only if you use really cheap beer.

As innings shoot by, pacing becomes essential. If you leave too much beer for the bottom half of an inning, you risk a rapid chug if the inning ends quickly — the double plays can be devastating. Extra innings can be catastrophic. Doubleheaders? Don't even think about it.

Luckily for beer-gamers, unforeseen lulls occur in any game: an extended manager-umpire confrontation, or a little rain, for example. Without breaks like these, only the "Seventh Inning Wretch" keeps **Beer-an-Inning** players in the game and cheering.

34.
Shot a Minute

Boot Factor: 4

Anyone who entertains the idea of doing a shot of beer every minute for an hour is truly a gaming enthusiast. **Shot a Minute** is that simple: each player has one minute to consume a one and one-half ounce shot of beer, and he must do so every minute for a full hour. No sweat, huh? Guess again, big guy.

For those who think **Shot a Minute** is for wimps, there's **The Century Club**: players drink a one ounce shot of beer every minute for 100 minutes. This works out to over eight beers per person, which does not appear to be so strenuous. But anyone who tries it will know differently. To make it especially tough, don't allow anyone to go to the bathroom until the game is over.

"I drink, therefore I am."

— Anonymous
(from H.L. Mencken's Quotes, page 311)

35.
Yards

Boot Factor: 4

Yards resembles a method of medieval torture more than a beer game. It pits the contestant against the clock to see who can drink a yard of beer the fastest.

A yard is 36 ounces of beer. The glass itself has a bowl at the bottom and a long, fluted neck. This design makes it particularly hard to drink the last few ounces of beer without pouring it all over yourself, an error that necessitates a penalty drink.

Several techniques have been developed to alleviate this problem. The most popular is to spin the yard slowly as you drink. The other is a method developed by the legendary "Boot" Strapp, who could consume a yard in six seconds. Strapp jammed the open end of the yard glass totally into his mouth and then simply opened his throat. His technique is generally acknowledged as the most effective. It has, however, never been duplicated.

Normal people will require anywhere from 15 to 30 seconds to drink the 28 ounces in a half-yard. A full-yard will take a good bit longer because the glass is much more difficult to handle.

Incidentally, **Yards** is considered *the* fraternity punishment to deal with unruly brothers.

A yard glass

36.
Caps

Boot Factor: 4

Caps ranks so high on the college popularity scale it is more accurately labelled an intramural sport. Though the concept is simple — throw a bottle cap in a beer to cause your opponent to drink — the effects can be devastating.

Two opponents sit face-to-face on the floor, legs in front and spread apart. Your feet must touch your opponent's feet, forming a diamond-shaped playing area. Next, a cup filled with beer is placed a few inches in front of each player's crotch. One contestant then throws a bottle cap in any fashion and tries to make it land in his opponent's cup.

If the throw is successful, the loser chugs one third or one half of his beer. If the cap hits the rim of the cup but does not go in, it is rethrown. Three rim-shots on any one turn, and the tosser must forfeit his throw and take a penalty drink. After a successful throw, you can play one of two ways. Either the winner gets to toss again, or the loser tosses.

Games are traditionally played to 11, 15, or 21 points and are always "win by two." You may lean as far forward as you can, but *no bending the knees*. If Moses Malone challenges you to a quick game of **Caps**, we advise you to decline respectfully.

Numerous tossing styles exist, but only three are consistently successful: backhand, freestyle, and the slam dunk. Defensively, your ability to wiggle your pelvis in an obscene fashion, hoot and holler, and make utterly foolish faces often proves effective in distracting opponents during their toss. Also important is knowing when to move the cup; it can be placed anywhere inside the playing "diamond."

In any case, when a full cup appears on the playing field, you should always throw with excessive velocity in order to splash beer all over your opponent's groin. This always makes for a good laugh.

37.
Acey-Deucey

Boot Factor: 4

Acey-Deucey is a typical beer game: moronically easy and a whole lot of fun. All you need is a deck of cards, beers, and some thirsty players.

To begin, the dealer gives each player two cards, face up. The player then bets one, two, or three shots of beer against the dealer that the third card will be in between the first two.

For instance, if the player has a three and a seven, he would have to draw a four, five, or six to win. Since the odds of doing this are not great, he would probably only bet one or two shots. If the player wins, the dealer must immediately do the shots. If the player loses, he drinks. Needless to say, a contestant only deals if he is really thirsty.

It must be noted that the first player decides whether aces are high or low. His decision dictates the status of the ace for the rest of the round. Also, if two successive cards are dealt (e.g., a six and a seven), the player must drink a shot.

Ten Spots To Leave Your Lunch

1. mailbox
2. hanging plant
3. sock drawer (not your own)
4. glove compartment
5. laundry chute
6. dog bowl
7. fish tank
8. golf bag
9. Cuisinart
10. through a sunroof (either direction)

38.
Hi-Lo

Boot Factor: 4

The next three games — **Hi-Lo, Red-Black**, and **Dimes** — were all developed in direct response to criticism that beer games are too complicated for the hopelessly drunk. Well, for those never-say-die partiers,**Hi-Lo** is the answer.

Hi-Lo requires only that players be able to recognize shapes and colors. It is played with a deck of cards divided evenly between the competitors. Each player turns over one card at a time. Those with low cards drink for every card higher than theirs.

For example, if three people are playing, the player with the lowest card drinks twice, the player with the middle card drinks once, and the player with the highest card does not drink at all. Ties are settled by suit: in order, Spades, Hearts, Diamonds, Clubs.

If this does not sound too complicated, even for the incredibly trashed, just wait till they try to shuffle. This task usually proves much too difficult, and the game ends.

"Show me a nation whose national beverage is beer, and I'll show you an advanced toilet technology."

— Mark Hawkins
The New York Times, Sept. 25, 1977

39.
Red Black

Boot Factor: 4

Even simpler to play than Hi-Lo is **Red Black**. It is the easiest beer game to learn and teach, and it's the quickest game to play. Thus, it is ideal when you need a game to pass the time between classes, while waiting for a date, during TV commercials, etc.

Two players place a deck of cards face down and draw from the top. If the card is red, you drink. If it's black, your opponent drinks.

It does not take a genius to realize that there are 26 red cards and 26 black cards in a deck. This means that each player will drink 13 beers during his trip through the deck (if traditional half-beer penalties are observed). If your competitive instinct demands that there be a winner, remove one card before starting.

"Beer is not a good cocktail-party drink, especially in a home where you don't know where the bathroom is."

— Billy Carter
Newsweek, Nov. 14, 1977

40.
Dimes

Boot Factor: 4

Dimes, played long enough, will make small change of both players. There's no disguising your purpose here. You want to get trashed and you want it now. With **Dimes**, the Power Drunk is no problem.

Luckily, the game is ridiculously simple. One of two players claims heads or tails and flips three dimes so that they land on the table. For every coin that comes up in his favor, his opponent must drink a shot glass full of beer. For every losing coin, the tosser drinks. Players alternate tossing. We're talking minimal strategy here.

Strange as it may seem, **Dimes** works equally well with quarters, nickels, and pennies.

"I will make it a felony to drink small beer."
— William Shakespeare
Henry VI, Part II

41.
Beer Pong

Boot Factor: 4

Traditionally, Ping-Pong has been associated with adroit Chinese and low-budget resorts. The mere addition of beer, however, transforms the game into a far more rewarding pursuit.

Beer Pong begins with each player placing his full cup on the center line of the table, about one foot from the back edge. The players flip a coin to see who will serve, and play commences with the normal Ping-Pong rules in effect (21 points per game, "win by two," best two out of three games, etc.). During rallies, each player tries to hit the other's cup with the ball. Players whose cups are struck must drink a certain amount depending on how and where the cup was hit.

There are four sips per cup, and the penalties are as follows:

Infraction:	*Drink Penalty:*
hit side of cup after bounce or on fly	one sip
hit rim of cup after bounce or on fly	two sips
hit cup on serve	server drinks two sips
ball lands in cup after bounce	three sips
ball lands in cup on fly	chug rest of beer
ball knocks cup over (fly or bounce)	refill cup and chug
player knocks own cup over	refill cup and chug
loser of game to 21 points	chug full beer

Remember, if a ball hits or bounces off any part of the cup and has *not* bounced on the table more than once, it is still in play. This rule creates the chance for multiple penalties on any single point. In such a case, the penalties are served in the order they occurred. Note that it is illegal to hit the opponent's cup on the serve, and net play to protect your own cup is really wimpy.

Beer Pong for doubles is identical to singles except that two cups per team are used. Players should place their cups one foot from the table's edge and one foot from either side of the center line. The players on each team must alternate returning the opponents' shots as they rally.

As play continues and brain cells discontinue, memory and motor coordination atrophy. But Pong athletes should still try to remember one or two effective shots. One is the drop shot which lands just over the net and dies. It often causes the opponent to lunge for the return, upsetting his own beer in the process. Another strategic shot is the deep lob, as it is a likely candidate to drop in the opponent's cup. But be careful — if the lob is played too short, you risk a punishing return and a beer *tsunami* (that's "tidal wave" for those of you at Ohio State). Bring many kimonos to clean up the mess.

"There is nothing wrong with sobriety in moderation."

— John Ciardi
The Saturday Review, Sept. 24, 1966

42.
Volley Pong

Boot Factor: 4

Volley Pong is a tougher form of Beer Pong that was developed, we suspect, by the Dartmouth fraternity system. We tried it up there on a football weekend and nearly lost our tacos. Fortunately, our football team fared better.

The game is for doubles only. Two cups of beer are placed side-by-side (touching) on the center line of the Ping-Pong table, approximately one foot from the back edge. Flip a coin to see who gets to receive first. Serving is a disadvantage. If a player hits the other team's cup on the serve, his team must take a pair of healthy gulps.

Once the serve is properly in play, the action more closely resembles volleyball than Ping-Pong. The receiving player "sets" or hits the ball into the air towards his teammate, who then slams or "spikes" the ball in the direction of the opponent's cups. If he misses but still hits the table, the other team can retrieve and volley in the same manner. But if they can't handle the slam and miss the ball, then they must serve. If the slamming player misses the table altogether, his team must serve. Should he hit the cups, the other players must down one-third of their beers. In the event that one or both cups are knocked over, the players must refill their beers, drink them, and wipe up the mess. All games are to 21, win by two, and Mung Rags are a must.

Twenty-Five Movies To Drink To: A Few Mindless Classics

1. Animal House
2. Fast Times at Ridgemont High
3. The Rocky Horror Picture Show
4. The Creature From the Black Lagoon
5. The Graduate *(not mindless, but great anyway)*
6. Halloween
7. Porky's
8. the pilot for "The Love Boat"
9. How To Stuff a Wild Bikini
10. Friday the 13th, Part II
11. The Endless Summer
12. Barbarella *(you remember — Jane Fonda in a see-through spacesuit)*
13. Spring Break
14. Caddy Shack
15. Eraserhead
16. Plan 9 From Outer Space
17. Enter the Dragon
18. Casablanca
19. Santa Claus Conquers the Martians
20. Apocalypse Now *(only if you leave before Brando starts quoting T. S. Eliot)*
21. any Tarzan movie with Johnny Weismuller
22. any James Bond movie *(Sean Connery preferred)*
23. any Clint Eastwood movie
24. any Ronald Reagan movie
25. Mars Needs Women

43.
Blow Pong

Boot Factor: 4

Blow Pong is the only beer game that should be considered for Olympic competition. Few games are as well-suited for settling heated rivalries: frat against frat, boys against girls, communists against capitalists.

The object of **Blow Pong** is to blow a Ping-Pong ball off the side of a table guarded by another team, thus forcing them to drink. **Blow Pong** boasts an enticingly high Boot Factor, based on the punishing combination of imbibition and hyperventilation.

The first step in **Blow Pong** is to prepare the equipment. Preferably, you should remove the net on a Ping-Pong table and tape the table's seam in order to provide a uniform rolling surface. Otherwise, use any fairly large table. Next, get a supply of Ping-Pong balls, and choose two teams. Each team claims a long and short end of the table to defend and kneels down around it accordingly. The ball is then dropped from a few inches above the center of the table, and blowing ensues. The team which blows the ball off its opponents' side scores a point. The scored-upon team must drink a specified amount. A single game is played to 21, and a match is the best of 3 (or 5).

If there are not enough players to form two teams, we suggest you try one-on-one play. Each player chooses a place at the table and uses two bottles or cups to define his goal. The rules of play are otherwise identical to team play.

The God-given ability to blow forcefully for a long duration cannot be improved, short of learning to play the tuba, but certain techniques can be helpful. First, don't allow your cheeks to puff out, as this contributes to loss of lip control, which leads to spraying and sputtering. Aside from transmitting assorted social diseases, sputtering at the **Blow Pong** table is simply bad manners. Secondly, the power for the blow should come from low in the belly, creating a sensation not unlike that leading to a good heave.

And now a few words on **Blow Pong** etiquette. Only ball hogs lean over the table. Leaning is bush, therefore the rule against breaking the vertical plane of the table must be enforced. The best technique to avoid a "face fault" is to maintain chin contact with the table edge. Also, a team loses the point if the ball touches any part of a player. Since the lips and nose are the most commonly hit areas, touching the ball is known as getting "faced." Because **Blow Pong** is a gentleman's game based on a strict code of honor, a player hit by the ball is obligated to end the point immediately by confessing.

The key strategem in **Blow Pong** is to determine the weak link in the opponent's line of defense. Invariably, one opponent is a little too hammered, too inept, or too inexperienced to stop laughing uncontrollably. This person is instantly pegged as the "black hole," a player who literally sucks. A smart team will concentrate on wailing him into cosmic dust.

Blow Pong has an all-time All Star team, which includes Ethel Merman, Louis Armstrong, Puff the Magic Dragon, Billy Martin, Linda Lovelace, and Moby Dick. Feel free to send us any other nominations.

44.
Bladder Bust

Boot Factor: 4

Bladder Bust is as simple as The 100 Beer Club, and just as demented.

Any number of people sit in a closed room. Each must drink a bottle of beer every five minutes. The first person who leaves the room for any reason loses. The last person left in the room wins.

That's it. Sick, huh?!

Beer Trivia

Q: Which of the following American forefathers was a brewer by hobby or profession: Samuel Adams, William Penn, Thomas Jefferson, George Washington?

A: *They all were. Sam Adams was a brewer by profession. William Penn had brewing vats on his Pennsbury estate. George Washington brewed his own at Mount Vernon. Thomas Jefferson collected books on brewing, and with these volumes and others he formed the Library of Congress.*

Q: Which of the following cities brews the most beer: Olympia, Milwaukee, Los Angeles, St. Louis, Denver?

A: *Wrong. It's L.A.*

Q: Which ten states have the greatest per capita beer consumption?

A: *Nevada (7.8 beers per week per resident), Wisconsin (7.0), New Hampshire (6.8), Montana (6.7), Wyoming (6.6), Texas (6.5), Arizona (6.4), Hawaii (6.2), Washington, D.C. (6.0), Colorado (5.9)*

Q: Which ten states have the wimpiest per capita consumption?

A: *Utah (3.2 beers per week per resident), Alabama (3.5), West Virginia (3.8), Arkansas (3.8), Connecticut (3.9), North Carolina (4.0), Kentucky (4.0), Georgia (4.1), Tennessee (4.1), Mississippi (4.1)*

Boot Factor Five

If the B.F. 4 player lives close to the edge, the Boot Factor Five player has jumped. He accepts the fact that the Big Ralph is imminent. His only question is when to strategically employ the reverse drink in order to outlast fellow Neanderthals. Generally speaking, if a player does not voluntarily reverse drink, he will involuntarily barf later in the game. Such a gross *faux pas* merits immediate disqualification and, of course, a penalty chug.

Beer Hunter
Slush Fund
Kill the Keg
Tending the Teat
The 100 Beer Club
Boot-a-Bout

Robert DeNiro in The Deer Hunter.

45.
Beer Hunter

Boot Factor: 5

Beer Hunter is truly hard-core. The game recreates the intensity of the classic Russian roulette scenes in the movie about Vietnam veterans, *The Deer Hunter*. Hence the name.

To simulate the ambiance of the smokey, back-room gallery in Saigon, Oriental music should be played softly in the background. Players should dress in Marine grunt fatigues and use rolled bandanas or neckties as headbands. The game should be approached with utter seriousness. It will get hysterical very soon.

The two players are led into the room blindfolded, and they are placed facing each other at a table. The referee then, with great fanfare, shows the spectators a new six-pack of beer. He removes each beer from its ring and places them all on the table between the players. He then takes one of the cans and shakes it up very hard. He places this can back on the table amongst the unshaken cans, and he switches the cans around so that no spectator knows which one is loaded. If they wish to do so, the spectators may now bet beer on which player will "survive."

When the betting is over, the referee removes the players' blindfolds and asks one of them to choose a can from the "ammo dump." The referee then spins this can on the table, and whichever player the top of the can is pointing to must go first. The player picks up the can, places it directly under his nostrils, and pulls the top. If the player hesitates before pulling the top, the judge must berate the player by yelling "Mao! Mao!" at him. If the player pulls the top and discovers that he does not have the loaded can, he then places his beer down, and his opponent must choose from the five remaining cans and repeat the procedure.

This intense activity continues until one of the players commits nasal suicide (i.e., gets the shaken can) and drenches himself. This losing player must drink the rest of his "loaded" beer, and then leave the table to work on drinking all the other beers that were opened in that round.

The surviving player is then re-blindfolded, and another contestant is led into the room, also blindfolded. The referee repeats the above procedure with another six-pack, and the new round begins.

Beer Hunter, of course, can be modified to accommodate up to six players. Remember, the loser must drink *all* open beers.

Obviously, **Beer Hunter**, like the movie, is a game suited only to those with nerves of steel. Those who hesitate will face a barrage of "Mao's!" from the referee, and that is probably more disgraceful than losing. Also, of course, **Beer Hunter** should be played with small cans of beer, since few could survive the explosion of a 12-ounce monster.

And remember, all those who play **Beer Hunter** will get wet. Very wet. But the sensation of beer-sodden clothes and the smell of stale brew against your skin usually serve to exhilarate the true beer hunter, making him feel as though he has survived a desperate battle against the commies and won. The clothes should be worn with undying pride long into the night.

46.
Slush Fund

Boot Factor: 5

Being dedicated gamblers, we decided there should be some way to play beer games and win money at the same time. Thus, we took it upon ourselves to create **Slush Fund**.

In **Slush Fund**, players must pay to drink. To begin, someone gets a full pitcher and everyone gathers around a table. Whoever starts must buy the privilege of drinking by dropping a quarter into the pitcher. He then drinks whatever amount he chooses right from the pitcher — glasses are too civilized for this game. After drinking, he passes the pitcher to the next player, who must also ante-up, and he, too, can drink as much as he wishes.

At any time, anyone who has possession of the pitcher can decide to take all the money at the bottom. All he has to do is finish the pitcher.

The strategy of the game quickly becomes obvious. Each drinker who decides *not* to pursue the money will drink as little as possible. The quarters will accumulate, and the pitcher will remain virtually full. Whenever someone decides to "drink for dollars," he will still have a very full pitcher to contend with. This intrepid player has decided that the accumulated fund is enough compensation for possibly having to "reverse drink" the pitcher minutes later.

Economics majors are usually stars at this game, with their keen sense of supply and demand. History majors, on the other hand, never seem to learn the lessons of the past.

47.
Kill the Keg

Boot Factor: 5

Kill the Keg is a ritual held at keg parties. It serves to separate the hearty quaffers from the lightweights and to polish-off unfinished kegs. After all, there is no excuse for leftover beer.

A round of **Kill the Keg** is called for when a keg party begins to die. This usually occurs at one of two times. Either the party becomes over-populated with the pompous cocktail set that finds verbal communication preferable to basic body language and heavy drinking (a practice utterly ill-suited to the beer blast). Or, the majority of guests have simply wimped-out, passed-out, or gone home. In either case, per capita beer consumption has fallen to embarrassing levels.

The call to "Rally!" is sounded, and **Kill the Keg** is born. A small group of strong-willed partiers gathers around the aluminum provider, and the players take turns filling their cups and drinking. Once a certain filling order is established, it may not be broken. Thus, as the last person in line fills up his beer, the first must have finished his and be ready to refill. This continues until the keg is dead. The keg should be continuously pumped to maintain a fast-pouring stream of beer.

The cardinal rules in **Kill the Keg** are that the tap must never be closed and that no beer can be spilled or wasted. The only way to slow the rate of consumption and give players a break to belch, breathe, and generally re-group is to add more players. As the game progresses and severe abdominal distension claims player after player, new recruits become the essential ingredient. But remember, it is *sacrilege* to close the tap.

If things get really rough, we suggest using the Heimlich Boot Maneuver on fellow players to make room for more beer.

48.
Tending the Teat

Boot Factor: 5

Tending the Teat is a feat requiring remarkable intestinal fortitude. To survive one round of **Tending the Teat** is to display one's true brew-swilling colors. It is a game, no, an *event*, in which participants go head-to-head with the stiffest competition imaginable: the keg. **Tending the Teat** is next of kin to Kill the Keg, but it is generally more daring, more heroic, more sicko.

To play **Tending the Teat**, a referee and an Honary Beer Wench must be chosen. The Wench is responsible for keeping the keg pumped so that beer flows out of the tap (the "teat") at a constant rate. The referee is responsible for presenting the rules, monitoring the game, announcing the winner, and providing artificial respiration.

The players gather around the keg, and the first player affixes his mouth to the tap. If the common, vertical tap is used, this may require some contortionist maneuvers to achieve relative comfort. Generally speaking, the sumo-wrestler, squat/straddle style seems to be most effective in achieving both comfort and maximum throat extension.

With the player in the ready position, the referee places two or three fingers lightly on the player's Adam's apple. The Maiden opens the tap, and the player swallows mouthful after mouthful, with the referee counting each gulp out loud as the drinker's Adam's apple bobs up and down. The point is to chalk up as many swallows as possible before drooling, snarfing, booting, or passing out. When the player can swallow no longer, he dismounts the keg and retires to the crowd to watch the next challenger.

When all contestants have had their fill, the referee announces the winner and brings — or drags — him in front of the cheering masses to be properly lauded.

49.

The 100 Beer Club

Boot Factor: 5

Membership in **The 100 Beer Club** is free and open to all. Although the requirements for admission are simple, few make the grade. All you need is a spare weekend and, oh, 100 beers or so. Got the idea?

Those warped enough to even consider joining the Club have from midnight Thursday until midnight Sunday to finish all one hundred 12-ounce beers. (After all, weekends were made for Michelob.) That works out to one beer every 43 minutes — if you stay awake for the duration. If you can count 100 empties at midnight on Sunday, and you have some witnesses to prove it, you are an official member of the Club. Of course, if you can even count on Sunday, you're doing pretty well.

Applicants to the Club perform best when they begin their quest with a large group of friends — that is to say, many friends, or simply large friends, like the football team. Peer pressure is very effective in keeping the drop-out rate low, though not much can be done about the pass-out rate. In any case, for those choosing to face this awesome task, discipline, a steady pace, and a physician's phone number are advised.

Since admission into **The 100 Beer Club** represents such high achievement, we want to formally recognize all members. Initiates should send us their names, brief details of their weekend (as much as they remember, anyway), and the names and addresses of some witnesses. Write to us in care of the publisher. An Honor Roll of the new members will be published in subsequent editions of this book.

50.
Boot-a-Bout

Boot Factor: 5

Boot-a-Bout is for animals — of course, we mean this as a compliment. In **Boot-a-Bout**, there are no winners. Players either lose their money or their lunch. Fortunately for exceptional players, it is possible at least to salvage your reputation.

The beauty of **Boot-a-Bout** lies in its simplicity. The game, which must be played in a bar, begins with one player buying a pitcher. He initiates the round by sipping from the pitcher and passing it to his right. The game continues like this, with each player drinking as much as he wants and then passing the pitcher.

There is only one rule, so read carefully: the player who drank just *before* the player who finishes the pitcher must buy the next pitcher, and start the next round.

If this sounds dull, think again. Many players will go to extraordinary lengths to avoid paying for the next pitcher. In fact, the pitcher rarely gets even half-empty before some proto-human goes for it. Some simians have been known to pound the whole pitcher right off the bat.

Of course, if you down the pitcher, you'll probably have to reverse-drink in the nearest bathroom if you want to play another round. Andre the Giant might be able to hold a quick pitcher or two in his estimable gut, but we mere mortals cannot.

A word about technique: an experienced **Boot-a-Bout** player knows just how much the person on his right can drink and how much he has drunk already. As this differential approaches zero, a good player will taunt the next player by drinking just enough of the pitcher to make it look tempting.

We recommend that everyone play **Boot-a-Bout** at least once in his life, just to know the anguish of clutching that three-quarters-full pitcher. Should you pass it? Is the guy next to you psyched to pound it? Or should you go for it? Do you really mind throwing up? Why are you doing this anyway?

Ah, such intensity of emotion is seldom felt these days. Of all beer games, only **Boot-a-Bout** brings on existential dilemmas. What prompts you to play such a game in a civilized world where no one is actually *making* you do it? Why do you barf when you don't have to? If these questions are as enigmatic to you as they are to us, then we suggest you head down to the local bar to play a few rounds of **Boot-a-Bout** tonight.

Twenty Post-Game Activities

1. Wear six-pack cartons like party hats.
2. Chow pizza.
3. Wake-up wimp roommates.
4. Go pickle-bobbing at the local deli.
5. Play air guitars.
6. Melt bottles in the fireplace.
7. Rearrange parked cars.
8. Steal road signs.
9. Break something you really didn't need.
10. Break something your roommate really did need.
11. Crank obnoxious music loud enough to disturb your neighbors.
12. Go cow tipping.
13. Have a fire extinguisher fight.
14. Men: Try to pick up girls at a party (while wearing #1, of course).
15. Women: Try to pick up guys at a party (also while wearing #1, of course).
16. See how much noise a keg makes bouncing down the stairs.
17. Sing off-key.
18. Prove the laws of gravity by throwing furniture out the window.
19. Blow chow.
20. Pass out.

Boot Factor 5 T-Shirt. (NOTE: This is a real item!) Be the first on your block to own an identical copy of the t-shirts worn by the famous beer authors during their extensive research tours. These stylish shirts are specially treated for beer, pretzel, and Lotria resistance. Nifty 4-hole design allows free movement of heads, arms, and torso. Mid-section even expands when you do! Four sizes: small, medium, large, and tub-o-lard. Makes an awesome gift! $9.95 (includes postage).

Monogrammed Caps. (NOTE: This is a real item!) Truly a mark of beer gaming distinction, these gold and silver painted caps are the perfect complement to every gamester's wardrobe. Perfect for those formal parties where regular caps are simply *declasse.* Our monogrammed caps combine ideal flight characteristics with stunning good looks. Monogram your caps with any three initials (your own intials, your fraternity or sorority, whatever). You'll want to throw these to your grandchildren someday. Set of three painted caps (specify silver or gold paint), with monogram and lovely case only **$12.95.** (includes postage).

You Can Help Us Find More Drinking Games.

Or you can turn the page...

This is a picture of starving authors. They are starving because they don't have any more beer games to write about. Pathetic, aren't they?

But we know that you, a true beer enthusiast, won't let them starve for long. We know that you will gladly share your knowledge of any obscure, hysterical games that the authors' extensive research efforts failed to uncover.

So, let us hear from you. If we use your game or suggestion in our next book (tentatively titled *Beer Games III: The Final Chapter*), we'll send you a free, autographed copy! Of course, if we don't use your game, you'll just get on another mailing list and get tons of junk mail. Write to:

Mustang Publishing, Inc.
Beer Research Dept.
P.O. Box 9327
New Haven, CT 06533

(All contributors will receive due recognition in the book, as well as a free autographed barf bag, or something equally nice. Your contribution is most likely not tax deductible, but you can give it a shot, anyway.)